MAPLE LEAF IN SPACE

MAPLE LEAF IN SPACE
Canada's Astronauts

JOHN MELADY

DUNDURN PRESS

TORONTO

Editor: Cheryl Hawley
Design: Jennifer Scott
Printer: Webcom

Library and Archives Canada Cataloguing in Publication

Melady, John
     Maple Leaf in space : Canada's astronauts / by John Melady.

Includes bibliographical references and index.
Issued also in an electronic format.
ISBN 978-1-55488-752-1

1. Astronauts--Canada--Biography--Juvenile literature. 2. Outer space--Exploration--Canada--History--Juvenile literature. I. Title.

TL789.8.C3M455 2011   j629.450092'271   C2010-902689-6

1   2   3   4   5   15   14   13   12   11

We acknowledge the support of the **Canada Council for the Arts** and the **Ontario Arts Council** for our publishing program. We also acknowledge the financial support of the **Government of Canada** through the **Canada Book Fund** and **Livres Canada Books**, and the **Government of Ontario** through the **Ontario Book Publishers Tax Credit** program, and the **Ontario Media Development Corporation**.

Care has been taken to trace the ownership of copyright material used in this book. The author and the publisher welcome any information enabling them to rectify any references or credits in subsequent editions.

J. Kirk Howard, President

Printed and bound in Canada.
www.dundurn.com

Dundurn Press	Gazelle Book Services Limited	Dundurn Press
3 Church Street, Suite 500	White Cross Mills	2250 Military Road
Toronto, Ontario, Canada	High Town, Lancaster, England	Tonawanda, NY
M5E 1M2	LA1 4XS	U.S.A. 14150

Mixed Sources
Product group from well-managed
forests, and other controlled sources
www.fsc.org Cert no. SW-COC-002358
FSC © 1996 Forest Stewardship Council

This book is for Alberta McNairn —
with my thanks for the suggestion you made almost 50 years ago

Contents

Introduction

This book is about the brave men and women who are Canada's astronauts. There are relatively few of them, but their contribution in their profession has been great. They have thrilled us, impressed us, and made us proud. They are achievers, risk takers, and yes, pioneers as well. Not so many years ago, there *were* no astronauts, and only characters in science fiction went into space. Not so today.

If you are a young person reading this book, you will learn just how unique our astronauts are. They do, and have done, memorable things. Hopefully you will too — if not in space, then in whatever occupation you choose. Our astronauts can be your personal role models, just as they have been for thousands of others.

1 A Spaceship Is Launched

By late afternoon, the spaceship *Endeavour* was ready to fly. It stood, tall and alone, dazzling and white, against the blue of the Florida sky. The fuel tanks were full, the final checks were done, the seven astronauts were strapped in and good to go. Over the loudspeakers, the countdown reached zero.

At first, nothing seemed to happen. But then, as the three powerful engines of the spaceship fired, the two solid rocket boosters roared to life, and in no time millions of litres of fuel became a white-hot firestorm. In those first milliseconds, the constraints that supported the shuttle were torn away, and it lurched above the gantry that had held it. As it did, the thousands of gallons of water that poured into the flame trench below the shuttle turned to steam that billowed in great white clouds over the launch pad and out to the sides. The water helped to lessen the shockwaves from the blastoff and insulated the pad from the extreme heat.

In the crew cockpit the astronauts felt the vibration and sensed the muffled roar of the machine that would hurl them to the heavens. Soon they would feel the crushing G-forces as the shuttle lurched higher and higher, tearing through the gravitational pull of the planet they call home.

Space shuttle launches are always dramatic. The white-hot flames from the great engines can be seen for miles, and the roar is ear-splitting. Here, spectators watch the early evening departure of Endeavour *on August 8, 2007. Canadian astronaut Dave Williams was on board.*

John Melady photo

Well back from the launch pad, in what is called the firing room, the technicians responsible for the flight relaxed slightly and breathed again. Now that their bird was flying they didn't have control over it anymore. Until its return, responsibility for the shuttle rested in faraway Houston, Texas. There, in a large, windowless room, before huge wall monitors and amid a sea of computers, the personnel of Mission Control would monitor every second of this flight. They would not be content until the spaceship was back, safe and secure on Earth again.

The launch of a space shuttle is terribly exciting and the interest it engenders never fades. The technicians responsible, the officials involved, the astronaut family members, and others who attend are not the only ones fascinated. People come from all over to watch. They cram all the viewing areas at the Kennedy Space Center (**KSC**), they park their cars along area roadsides, claim spaces on the nearby Atlantic beaches, and even pack into boats to get close to the action. In the last several years, millions of people of all ages have seen spaceships launched. If you ever get a chance to watch a launch, go. You will never forget it. Who knows, you may even be lucky enough to be there when a Canadian astronaut flies. And better still, one day perhaps one of the crew members might be you. That is not an impossible dream. Every astronaut who ever flew had the same dream.

Why would you go to Florida to see a launch? The answer is that you will see and experience a whole lot more than what you might see on the television news. You will hear the thundering roar as the spaceship starts its climb. You will feel the excitement of the occasion, and the happiness of those around you. You will find yourself laughing, cheer-

FASCINATING FACT
What Does the Word "Astronaut" Mean?

Astronaut is the combination of two Greek words. *Aster* means "star" and *naut* means "sailor." So literally translated, the word means "star sailor." Indeed, the men and women who fly into space seem to sail toward the stars.

ing, and applauding along with everyone else. And then, if you are close enough, you may even feel the shockwaves as they hit you. Certainly, you will be in awe as this rocket streaks higher and higher, until at last it is no more than a tiny dot against the far away sky.

Of course, the people who build the space shuttles, test them, prepare them for flight, transport them to the launch pads, and control them while they are in orbit have a lot to do before the big day. Thousands of people work at all these things, but it is the astronauts who we know best. They get to ride these rockets. We often see them on television during their training times, as they wave to the crowds just before launch, while they work at the International Space Station, or after their flight, when they are being interviewed by reporters.

Today, everything to do with spaceship design, development, and assembly is an international effort. Shuttle parts and space-related pieces of equipment are made all over Canada, but the best known are the Canadarms and that amazing invention called Dextre. We'll talk more about those later in the book. First, let's examine the major steps in the period that leads up to every launch.

In the weeks before a mission the shuttle is checked over, carefully and often, and sometimes more or less rebuilt, in order to ensure that it is as safe as possible for the fantastic

Before being moved out to a launch pad, all space shuttles are assembled on a mobile launcher platform inside the giant Vehicle Assembly Building at the Kennedy Space Center. The VAB is one of the largest buildings in the world, and can be seen for long distances in every direction.

John Melady photo

and dangerous journey to come. This important work is done in what is called the Orbiter Processing Facility at KSC. Then, once the experts there are sure the spaceship is flight ready, it is moved — ever so carefully — into the Vehicle Assembly Building (**VAB**), the largest structure of its kind in the world. In fact, the VAB is so big — 160 metres high — that it towers above everything else in that part of Florida. Its huge bulk is even visible to passing ships, far out on the Atlantic Ocean. The enormous weight of the thing rests on over 4,000 steel supports, or pilings, each 40 centimetres in diameter, and driven down 48 metres into the solid bedrock below. It was built strong enough to survive the high winds of hurricanes, and has done so several times.

If you visit the Kennedy Space Center when you are in Florida, you should take a tour, which will let you see the VAB close up. Its massive doors are opened each time a shuttle, its two solid rocket boosters, and the attached external fuel tank are moved to a pad prior to launch. The

FASCINATING FACT
What Is the VAB?

VAB refers to Vehicle Assembly Building. It is one of the largest buildings of its kind in the world, and towers above everything else in east-central Florida. This is the building where space shuttles are prepared for flight.

doors are opened at other times, of course, but the most dramatic occasion is when the shuttle is taken out. The doors themselves work like the garage doors on a house, but are enormous by comparison. In fact, they reach almost to the top of the VAB, where a large American flag has been painted — each one of its stripes wider than a highway bus! In fact, this flag, like the building it adorns, is one of the largest in the world.

But what actually happens in the Vehicle Assembly Building?

Not long before each shuttle is launched it is moved to the VAB. Once inside, it is slowly and carefully hoisted upwards until it seems to be sitting on its tail. Then the solid rocket boosters are bolted to its sides. Finally, the 47-metre-long external fuel tank is affixed to the belly of the shuttle. This entire process is slow and has to be done extremely carefully. Remember, the astronauts who will fly on the spaceship trust their lives to the men and women who prepare it for launch.

MAPLE LEAF IN SPACE

After many days of preparation and constant checking, the shuttle, the solid rocket boosters, and the external fuel tank are at last ready to go to the launch pad. All together, these components are known as "the stack," which has to be moved almost 5 kilometres to one of two launch pads, numbered 39A or 39B. But how?

For this journey, a machine called a crawler-transporter is used. This vehicle, like so many other components at Kennedy, is huge. It is also slow moving and very powerful. In a sense, it is like a great bulldozer without a front blade. It move on treads, like a bulldozer, and each link of each tread weighs about over 900 kilograms (2,000 pounds) and has 456 links.

To understand just how big the crawler-transporter is we'll compare it to a baseball diamond. They are about the same size, but the baseball diamond doesn't move. The crawler does

— but only at 1.6 kilometres per hour when its carrying a stack. It can move about twice that fast, but *never* when loaded. On the way out to the launch pad, this big, heavy, and very slow monster machine travels on what is called a crawlerway, a wide, two-lane gravel road. No cement or asphalt is used here because neither would support the combined 7,711,070 kilograms (17 million pounds!) that the stack and crawler weigh. Because it is about 5 kilometres from the VAB to a launch pad, it takes the crawler several hours to get there.

Finally, when everything is ready, the shuttle is launched. If all goes well, the astronauts on board will find themselves in space less than 10 minutes after they leave the Earth. As soon as they are in orbit, their dreams of being out of this world really come true.

A giant crawler-transporter moves a shuttle to the launch pad.
The crawler weighs nearly 3 million kilograms (6 million pounds).

NASA photo

2 Dogs and Monkeys Fly

We all know about such things as satellites, spaceships, shuttle launches, and landing on the moon. We see astronauts on television, dressed in bulky suits, working at the International Space Station, while in the background oceans, countries, and clouds drift past. Occasionally, these adventurers wave to the camera, but not often. That is because their focus is on their job. Most of the time we cannot see their faces, but we can sometimes get an idea of what they are doing. Generally, their movements seem awkward, jerky, deliberate, and slow.

But in one sense, they are not slow at all. Even though they must always work with particular care when they are in space, the astronauts are speeding around the globe every 90 minutes or so. For that matter, so is the space station. That is because both have become satellites, and their orbit is both predictable and accepted. But at the beginning of space exploration there were no astronauts, and the space station didn't exist. The only things in the skies were creatures that fly and the stars, planets, the moon, and so on. There were also airplanes, of course, but no satellites that had been made here on Earth. However, on Friday, October 4, 1957, that changed forever. Shortly before midnight, a small, silver-coloured, 83-kilogram (184-pound) mechanical ball was launched into space on a Russian rocket. About the size of a beach ball, the little device would circle the Earth more than

1,400 times before it disintegrated when it fell into the atmosphere of the Earth. It was the first satellite made by human beings.

The ball was called Sputnik.

The launch of this first satellite had a great impact on people everywhere — but no more so than in Russia and in the United States. Both of these countries were profoundly affected by the "little moon," as it was sometimes called. The Russians bragged because it was theirs; the United States worried because the Russians, who were America's rivals, had launched it. Almost immediately, the two became involved in a fierce competition to see which could launch bigger and better satellites, and be the first to send a rocket carrying a human being into space. The efforts of the two soon became known as the "Space Race," which lasted for several years. Canada was never directly involved.

There were many obstacles in the struggle for the skies. Everyone knew that even if rockets that were large and powerful enough to transport humans could be built they would need to be tested before anyone flew in one. For that reason, scientists began to look around for test animals that they could send first, to see if humans could survive the flight. Two different creatures were selected for the purpose: the Russians chose dogs; the Americans picked monkeys. These animals performed well, but sometimes with tragic consequences.

The first dog used by the Russians was a cute brown-and-white terrier that someone found wandering on a street in the city of Moscow. She was given the name *Laika*.

In order for her to be comfortable on her journey, a special compartment was built for Laika, inside another Sputnik. She was provided with food, water, and oxygen, and because she was a test animal, had to have sensors attached to her body so that the scientists would know how she was doing once the rocket carrying her took off.

At first, Laika was fine, and didn't seem to have any trouble adapting to

FASCINATING FACT
Where Did the Name *Laika* Come From?

Laika is a Russian word that translates to "Barker" in English. Laika was given her name because, even though she was gentle, she was excitable, curious, and loved to bark. Nevertheless, the technicians who prepared her for her journey grew quite attached to the stray mutt, as did dog lovers around the world who heard about the trip she was about to take.

the shock of being blasted into space. She circled the Earth several times, making her quite famous. People who knew nothing about satellites or rockets learned of Laika, and hoped she would have a good trip. Sadly, they would soon be disappointed.

No plans had been made to bring the poor little pooch back to Earth, and she died all alone, inside her tiny spaceship. That Sputnik burned up when it re-entered the Earth's atmosphere, like meteors do when they appear as shooting stars. Nevertheless, Laika gave her life so that humans could learn how to fly into space and survive the ride to get there. Because she helped to make that possible, Laika will always be remembered — both by the scientists who sent her, and by all those who heard of her and loved her.

Two other dogs, Chaika and Lisichka, should be remembered as well, even though they didn't get to go as far as Laika. They were placed inside a satellite, called Korabl-Sputnik, that was both larger and more advanced than the original Sputnik. At first the new capsule seemed to be as good as the technicians claimed, but soon guiding it became a problem. Shortly after it was launched, Korabl-Sputnik spun out of control and the rocket blew up within sight of the launch area, shocking the spectators on the ground. Neither the capsule nor its passengers survived — both dogs died instantly and the matter became another heartbreaking story of early space exploration. Fortunately, the next pair of dogs had more success. Their names were Strelka and Belka.

The spaceship carrying them left the Earth just three weeks after the previous rocket exploded. This time, the launch went according to plan and Strelka and Belka rode side by side into space. They were strapped into the compartment designed for them, and neither seemed uncomfortable, even with the sensors they had to wear. Two of these devices measured the heartbeat of each dog, so that the technicians back on Earth could tell if the wild ride caused discomfort. Fortunately, on this trip, there were no real problems. The newest space dogs spun around the world 17 times, then came safely back to Earth when the parachute carried on their satellite opened as intended. A day or so later, pictures of the two appeared in newspapers in many countries — including the United States. But by this time, scientists there were teaching a friendly, rather scruffy little monkey how to be an astronaut. His name was Ham.

The chimpanzee named Ham, being shown off by his trainer at Cape Canaveral, Florida.

NASA photo

The small beast was technically a chimpanzee, but to most people, he was simply a monkey. He would soon become just as famous as Laika, but unlike her, he survived his one and only flight. Most of the people who dealt with him liked him — or they did until he actually returned from space. But more on that later.

Ham was one of about 40 chimps the Americans collected for use as possible fliers. They were well-fed, and kept in a modern, clean compound where they could exercise and play. Technicians attempted to train several of them for space flight, but soon found that some in the group simply refused to co-operate. Others did well. When a blue light flashed, the smarter ones soon learned to push buttons and turn dials, because when they did so they got a reward — generally a banana pellet. And they all *loved* banana pellets! The less-intelligent chimps expected a reward, yet refused to do anything to earn it. Particularly stubborn members just sat and sulked.

Before long, the scientists who worked with the chimps realized that Ham was undoubtedly the brightest of all. He watched for the blue lights, then flipped the switches, turned the knobs, and pushed the buttons on a spaceship model, again and again without seeming to be either bored or tired. Each time he did what was expected he gulped down his banana pellet and begged for another.

Despite his obvious intelligence, as the time for his spaceflight grew closer and closer, the technicians thought that they might better have some kind of a backup system to ensure Ham did as they wanted. If he flipped the correct switches at the right time, he was rewarded. But the scientists wondered — suppose he suddenly decided he didn't want a pellet? If that happened, important things they wanted Ham to do would not get done. The backup was intended to force him to concentrate, and do what was required.

Small electrical footpads were made and installed in the model, while identical devices were placed in the real spaceship that Ham would fly. If he did the things he was supposed to do, he would get his pellet. If he failed to co-operate, he received electrical shocks to the soles of his feet. The shocks were not enough to injure him, but Ham hated them and worked as hard as he could to avoid them.

Unfortunately, when the big day came, the rocket that carried Ham into space was not launched correctly. For some reason, the angle of its flight was not what was intended, resulting in poor little Ham flying much farther than expected. His spaceship was supposed to come down by parachute in a particular area in the Atlantic Ocean, where several ships waited. But because Ham overshot the intended landing area, the nearest ship took quite some time to get to him to save him.

There were other problems, too. The rocket flew much faster than intended, creating more G-force and putting extra pressure on the chimp as he shot into space and again when he came down.

Then there was the problem of the blue lights. They didn't operate correctly, and Ham struggled to punch buttons, flip switches, and turn knobs — faster and faster until he was close

FASCINATING FACT
What Is G-Force?

G-force is short for "gravitational force." It can come from very large objects (like the Earth) or from acceleration. You know the feeling when you're in a car that suddenly speeds up and you get pushed back against your seat? That's G-force. If there was no gravitational force, we would drift off into space. The amount of gravitational force is measured in units called "g"s. One G is the amount of force that keeps us on the Earth. The best pilots in fighter jets can cope with 7 or 8g. But pilots are trained to tolerate high G-force and Ham didn't have any of this kind of training at all. Incredibly, he absorbed as many as 15g on his wild ride.

to exhaustion. All the while, the irritating shocks to his feet continued, sometimes even when he did what he was trained to do. Finally, and worst of all, when his capsule landed in the ocean, seawater poured in and almost drowned him.

Ham was trapped inside his little prison, and because of the speed of his flight he was far from the area where he was supposed to have been picked up. In fact, by the time the helicopter from a rescue ship got to him, both Ham and the capsule were thoroughly waterlogged and close to sinking. Luckily, the little chimp survived the ordeal — but was he angry!

When the rescuers opened the hatch of his spaceship, they soon learned that the half-drowned monkey was not a happy traveller. When someone went to unbuckle the safety straps that were holding him in place, Ham snarled, suddenly turned sideways and tried to bite the person trying to help him. He rolled his eyes, thrashed around, spit, and growled. Then he attempted to remove his restraints and grew even angrier when he realized he could not do so. He then sat there, bared his teeth, and almost dared anyone to come near him.

Eventually, his handlers got him calmed down, dried off, and safe in an enclosure aboard a ship. After a time, he rejoined the other chimps back at the facility built for them. And while Ham's career in space was over, he had proven to the Americans that they would now be able to send a human astronaut into space. In fact, in the space of a single month in 1961, both the Americans and the Russians did so.

3 Two Tragedies

As soon as Russia and the United States felt that they could send human beings into space and bring them back safely, the race to do so became intense. Each country wanted to be first. Russia was the winner. On April 12, 1961, the Russians launched a young pilot named Yuri Gagarin into space. He circled the Earth once and then came back down. The whole trip lasted 108 minutes. Three weeks later, on May 5, an American astronaut named Alan Shepard became the second man in space. He took off from Cape Canaveral, Florida, reached an altitude of 186.4 km and then landed in a particular location in the Atlantic Ocean. Both flights are regarded as very important ones.

Immediately following these missions, both nations continued building and launching improved spaceships. In the years that followed, many astronauts flew; alone and with others. Voyages became longer. Eventually, the idea of landing on the moon became irresistible. In fact, for a time it was the one destination everyone talked about. Finally, on July 20, 1969, two Americans landed there and walked its surface, ensuring that the United States won the overall space race. In time, the Americans made more landings on the moon, yet even today only 12 human beings have ever been there.

While going into space has always been a great adventure, it is also an extremely dangerous one. Dogs and monkeys died in accidents and, sadly, humans did too. The best known accidents are the American tragedies.

The first accident occurred on the ground. On the morning of January 27, 1967, three astronauts were testing a capsule. In order to make the test as realistic as possible, the entry hatch had been sealed. A sudden electrical spark touched off an explosion inside the capsule and the men perished before they could be rescued. The event was heartbreaking, but the manufacturers of the spaceship, the technicians at Kennedy, and those in charge learned from what had happened, and made several corrections in the hope that no one else would die on the job.

But despite their best efforts, accidents happen.

The second disaster came much later, when a shuttle, one of the large airplane-like spaceships, blew apart just after it had been launched. Seven brave men and women died as a crowd of spectators watched.

That morning the weather in central Florida was extremely cold. In the area around the KSC, where the United States launches all of its manned spaceships, orange and lemon trees had frost on their branches. The alligators in an adjacent wildlife refuge seemed to know it was too cold to sun themselves. They lay in reeds and waterways and stayed out of sight. No one swam at any of the beaches that are not far from KSC, and people out walking wore jackets and complained of the cold.

On the huge, cement and steel support structure, or launch pad, where the shuttle, the *Challenger*, waited for launch time, long icicles hung from metal beams. The workers who readied the shuttle for flight saw the ice and urged their bosses to delay the takeoff until the weather improved. A delay, or hold, was decided upon, and what is called the countdown to launch was stopped for a time. But not long enough.

After a couple of hours delay, the shuttle was launched. It began to soar from the launch pad into the cold blue of the Florida sky. Thousands and thousands of people watched, all of them excited, hopeful, and happy that they were there to see this flight. But they were horrified by what happened above their heads. The *Challenger* had only flown for 73 seconds when

The vapour trail left by the space shuttle Challenger *when it blew up. Thousands of people watched the launch at the Kennedy Space Center in Florida.*

NASA photo

something went terribly wrong with it. Parts began to fall off, and then the entire machine exploded in a tremendous mass of fire and smoke.

The crew cabin and the rockets that propelled the spaceship flew on for a few seconds. More and more of the shuttle broke apart and fell, and soon the only indication of where it had been was a smoke smear in the cloudless sky. Most people who were there continued to look upwards, but even as they did they knew the men and women who flew that day were dead. Across the Kennedy Space Center grounds there was shock and tears. The tragedy was hard to accept for everyone, but particularly for the many family members who watched their loved ones perish.

Despite the improvements that the *Challenger* commission brought about, there has been one more major disaster in the American space program. On February 1, 2003, the shuttle *Columbia* was lost after it had been in flight for 15 days and had travelled around the Earth 255 times. Seven more astronauts died in an accident that was just as dramatic and terrible as the loss of the *Challenger*. Millions of people in many countries saw what happened on television.

The shuttle was on its way home from space when the end came. However, the problem started much earlier — on the day *Columbia* was launched.

In the great flash and roar that occurs as shuttles leave the pad they vibrate wildly, and often small bits and pieces of debris fall from them. However, as *Columbia* thundered upward, a rather large, briefcase-sized chunk of insulating foam broke off the external fuel tank, and a split second later knocked a

FASCINATING FACT
Aftermath of the *Challenger* Disaster

After the *Challenger* was lost the entire space program was put on hold while a special commission determined the cause of the accident. The commission, which was chosen by then-President Ronald Reagan and included Neil Armstrong (the first man to walk on the moon), determined that the accident was caused by a combination of the cold and a design flaw that allowed hot gases to travel between two chambers in the *Challenger*'s engine, leading to the explosion that destroyed the shuttle. After the results of the inquiry were released the remaining shuttles were redesigned to fix the flaw and a new system was to help the crew escape in the event of emergencies during takeoff. It was also decided that no more launches would take place in such cold weather. The shuttle program resumed over a year-and-a-half later when shuttle *Discovery* was launched on September 29, 1988.

piece of tile loose. The tile is like an external skin that protects the shuttle during re-entry to Earth, when outside temperatures can reach almost 1700 degrees Celcius. Unfortunately, because of the loosened tile, when *Columbia* streaked through the atmosphere on the way home, hot gases were sucked inside through a hole under the left wing. As soon as that happened, the spaceship was doomed.

Flight directors at Mission Control in Houston knew immediately that something was wrong. Up until that time, they had been in close radio contact with the pilot of *Columbia* and everything seemed to be going well. The spaceship was on course, and in a short time it would be landing as scheduled in Florida. But conversation with the pilot ended abruptly. Mission Control called the shuttle again and again, but there was no reply. In fact, what had been a magnificent flying machine was breaking apart, and falling in thousands of pieces across a wide band of countryside in the southwestern United States.

By this time, everyone on board *Columbia* was dead.

Once again there was an investigation into what had happened, and several flights were postponed until problems could be corrected. Following the loss of *Columbia*, lots of attention was given to the state of the tiles that protect the shuttles. It was decided that they should be inspected during each mission. This was done on the very next flight, and has been on every mission since.

American spaceships are not the only ones that have had accidents. The Russians have had their difficulties as well. Unfortunately, Yuri Gagarin was killed in the crash of a jet plane, but he will always be remembered as the first man in space. Other Russians have died too. In one case, three men were returning to Earth when the air leaked out of their spaceship. Without oxygen to breathe they all died. When a ground crew reached the capsule after it had come down by parachute, they said the three looked as though they had simply fallen asleep. They didn't seem to have been aware of what was about to happen. Another Russian pilot died on the ground, in an accident that was very similar to the capsule fire that killed three Americans. Again, pure oxygen ignited in a test chamber and a flash fire caused his death. Even though the investigations that followed each of these accidents led to various improvements in spaceship design and precautions for launches, going to space is, and always will be, dangerous.

Yet it is something many want to do.

Each and every time astronauts are being hired, far more people apply than there are positions. This has always been a fact in the United States and Russia, and now in other countries as well. Here in Canada, thousands applied on the three occasions when our government decided Canadian astronauts were needed. Men, women, and even boys and girls put their names forward, although many probably knew they had no real chance of being selected. However, once all the names were in, every application was evaluated by a panel of experts and the best candidates were picked. Today, at least one of our astronauts helps in the selection of new members.

In order to have a chance of becoming an astronaut, those applying must be unique individuals. They have to be university graduates who are creative, industrious, intelligent, and they must be able to work well with others. In this country, preference is given to Canadian citizens who are scientists, doctors, or engineers. Those selected must be physically fit and in excellent health because the jobs they will be doing are extremely demanding. All of our astronauts are highly qualified and all of them have been wonderful representatives for Canada.

4 A New Kind of Spaceship

One of the best ways to become an astronaut is to stay in school and work hard. But even then there are no guarantees that the job will be yours. It is a highly selective, skilled profession, and only a few get to enter it. Education alone is not enough. While all astronauts have to be good in school, and in math and science particularly, they also must work well with others, be outgoing, and be determined.

Every one of Canada's astronauts possesses these traits, and more. They can fly aircraft, solve complicated technical problems, speak French and English fluently, and parachute from planes. All are good athletes, effective public speakers, skilled organizers, and successful at handling stress.

They come from varied backgrounds: from the country and from the city, from big families and small, from homes where achievement was important and hard work praised. To date, no Canadian astronaut was raised in an extremely wealthy home; on the other hand, none came from poverty. All came from backgrounds where education was important. None were failures in school.

Several, even when they were in elementary school, dreamed of becoming astronauts when they grew up. There were lots of reasons for this: they watched spaceships liftoff on television, they saw men walking on the moon, they talked to astronauts who came to their school and described the job. But since flying in a spaceship is a fairly new profession, none had a mother or father who was an astronaut.

When they were kids, some of our astronauts built pretend spaceships; others collected pictures of astronauts instead of hockey cards. Many kept scrapbooks about space flight, and one or two had autographs of astronauts. Some clipped magazine and newspaper stories that mentioned their heroes.

Every one of Canada's astronauts is an adventurer at heart. They all love challenges — the idea of exploring, of learning, and of finding ways to achieve success in the face of difficulty.

The space shuttle Atlantis *returns from a successful mission. Because the shuttle operates like a glider for the landing it* must *touch down on the first attempt.*

NASA photo

They truly go where few have gone, they see what most never see, and they experience the exhilaration of being weightless as the spaceships they ride speed toward the stars.

To date, all of our astronauts have gone into space on one or more of the shuttles, or on a Russian Soyuz vehicle. Originally, the United States flew machines with names like Mercury, Gemini, and Apollo. The familiar shuttles only began to fly after the last Apollo mission was over. All of the men who went to the moon did so during the Apollo era. In Russia, the spaceships were called Vostok, Voskhod, and Soyuz. Over time, both Americans and Russians built space stations. Today, the large International Space Station (**ISS**) was constructed by men and women from several countries. Canada is one of them.

Because the shuttles used by the United States are so important, let's take a look at this marvelous machine. At first glance it looks like an airplane, but it is much more than that. It is launched in an upright position, like a rocket, with its front end facing the sky. Later, when it returns to Earth, the shuttle lands like a glider. And because it operates like a glider, it cannot attempt to land and then circle around for another try if the first approach is wrong. It glides back to Earth because the big engines used on liftoff were not designed for a powered landing. All shuttle pilots are really good at their job, but they know they *must* land correctly the first time or risk a crash.

The first space shuttle flew in the spring of 1981, with two astronauts on board. They were the commander and the pilot. There is no co-pilot on any shuttle. The trip was really an experimental one. Everyone involved with this new kind of spaceship wanted to see how well it worked.

FASCINATING FACT
The Shuttle Launch Pads

There are two shuttle launch pads at the Kennedy Space Center in Florida. They are Pad 39A and Pad 39B. Both have huge towers, or gantries, built on elevated platforms. Before being launched, shuttles rest on these platforms, and are under guard 24 hours a day. At night, very powerful search lights illuminate both the pad and the shuttle that stands on it.

Fortunately, the two-day flight was successful. At the end of the trip, because no shuttle had ever landed before, an extra-long runway was used. This was on a dry lake bed in California. The first shuttle was called *Columbia*, and during the next several years it made many trips. In all, five shuttles have flown, all of them numerous times.

MAPLE LEAF IN SPACE

Today, there are generally seven astronauts on each flight. In addition to the commander and pilot, most of the other crew members are called mission specialists. They are highly trained and have specific jobs to do once the spaceship is en route. In later sections of this book, these jobs will be described in detail.

The shuttle's measurements are generally given in Imperial numbers, and all five are the same size. By itself the machine is just under 57 feet high, 122 feet long, with a 78-foot wingspan (that's about 17 metres high, 37 metres long, and a 24-metre wingspan). The crew module, where the astronauts ride, is in the front of the shuttle; the middle contains the cargo bay, or payload bay; and the three main engines are at the back. The payload bay is a huge part of the spaceship — big enough that a school bus would fit inside it. This area has to be large in order to transport the kinds of cargo launched on the various missions.

The front part of the shuttle is undoubtedly the most interesting and the most important. That is because the cockpit is there, as are the flight controls, the communication system, the galley (kitchen), the crew living quarters, the washroom, and the seats used by the astronauts during launch and landing. The shuttle, which is also called the orbiter, is probably the most complex piece of machinery ever made. It has millions of parts — and *all* of them have to be in proper working order before every launch.

There is not much room in the front part of the shuttle, and even that area is divided. The top section, or flight deck, is where the commander and pilot fly the spaceship, make course corrections, and do all the other things that have to be done on every mission. The controls are there for handling whatever is in the payload bay, as are the ones needed for docking the shuttle at the International Space Station. In all, there are over 2,000 individual switches, knobs, levers, and displays in this part of the orbiter. There are 10 windows, and total seating capacity is four.

A small opening in the flight-deck floor leads directly down to the mid-deck, an area about 4.5 metres long and 4 metres wide. That's where other crew members spend a great deal of time. In the galley, they prepare their meals. These are vacuum packed, and are some- times even tasty. Food on the early missions was not very good, but improvements have been made since then. There are sleeping stations on the mid-deck, as well as storage spaces. The only window is a small round one in the entry/exit hatch. That's why, when astronauts want

John Melady photo

The commander's seat and flight-deck interior of a space shuttle. Extensive electronic upgrades have been made to all of the shuttles. The first one that flew was Columbia, STS-1, on April 12, 1981.

to get the best view of the world they are flying over, they prefer to go up to the flight deck to do so. Below the mid-deck is space for storage.

The payload bay makes up the large midsection of the shuttle. Here, both big and small items are carried. Today, most of this cargo goes to the International Space Station, but there have been lots of other items transported as well. Many of the satellites that circle the Earth were taken into space on the shuttles. The large and marvelous Hubble Telescope was one of them. As well, very sophisticated science laboratories fit inside the cargo bay. The best known is called Spacelab, where astronauts have done important scientific work that has applications here on Earth, as well as in space. Entry into the Spacelab is through a tunnel from the crew module. Once inside the lab, the astronauts have a much larger area to work, rather than being cramped at the front for an entire mission. During launch and landing though, all are strapped in their assigned seats in either the cockpit or the mid-deck.

The three shuttle engines at the rear of the spaceship are absolutely necessary for the proper launch of the craft. All are big: over 2 metres wide and 4 metres long, and they each weigh almost 3,175 kilograms (7,000 pounds). That's about twice as much as a small car weighs. The fuel they burn is a mixture of liquid hydrogen and liquid oxygen, which is carried in a large, 47-metre-long orange fuel tank. The engines themselves operate for less than 10 minutes, the time it takes for the spaceship to go from the launch pad to orbit.

The fuel necessary to get the shuttle into space is consumed at a rate that is almost impossible to imagine. In *less than half a minute*, the amount burned would drain a fairly large backyard swimming pool!

But the three engines do not provide all the power. On either side of the spaceship are things called solid rocket boosters. These machines are truly rockets, and they and the shuttle are bolted together for the launch. The boosters only operate for the first two minutes of the flight though, just long enough to help blast the shuttle toward the skies. After those two minutes, they separate from the spaceship and then come down by parachute into the Atlantic Ocean. There they are picked up by workers in boats, and are used again and again.

Once the main engines and the solid rocket boosters have done their work, the space shuttle enters orbit. There, flying between 160 and 645 kilometres above the Earth, it circles the globe, alone, or docked at the space station. As soon as the shuttle enters orbit the men and women on board become weightless, allowing them to go about their duties in an entirely different and wonderful way. It is then that they are particularly pleased they decided to become astronauts. If you were among them, you would share their joy.

5 Where Astronauts Train

Shortly after they have been selected, all new astronauts begin a period of training that is as rigorous as any on Earth. However, before that happens, they are interviewed by reporters, their pictures appear in magazines and newspapers, and they answer questions on television and radio news shows. And while most Canadians only know them through the media, in the places where they were born, grew up, or went to school, they are often celebrities. A successful applicant from a small town is particularly important to the people there, and from the day of the selection, his or her career is followed with interest. That career begins at Houston, a big American city in the state of Texas.

A short distance outside that city is a huge enterprise called the Johnson Space Center. There are over 100 buildings there, some huge, some not. Taken together, they resemble a large university campus, but instead of going to school to take all the usual subjects, the student astronauts are there to prepare to fly in space, work in space, and survive in that dangerous and unique environment.

There is nowhere else that is quite like this location. For many years now, young astronauts, and many not so young, have gone there. All were changed by the experience. Some

The Apollo era Mission Control Center in Houston. This was the control room used for all of the early space flight operations, including the moon landings and the flights of the first Canadian astronauts. It is now a designated historic site.

John Melady photo

FASCINATING FACT
History of Johnson Space Center

The Johnson Space Center was first opened in 1961. Originally, it was named the Manned Spacecraft Center, but in 1973 it was renamed in honour of the late U.S. President Lyndon B. Johnson. The center sits on 656 hectares (1,620 acres) of land and includes 100 buildings. The center is located near Houston because the area fulfilled all of NASA's requirements at the time, which included a mild climate, at least 1,000 acres of land, and being close to water that didn't freeze over, an airport that was open year round, a Department of Defense (DoD) air base with runways for military jet aircraft, and a university.

left before they ever flew, others left after going into space one or more times, some "washed out," or failed in the training they had to take. Many simply decided that they didn't want to be astronauts after all, so they said goodbye to their classmates and left. Others came back for additional training, or because they had particular skills they could pass along to others.

Johnson Space Center, often referred to as "Houston," is where the missions to the moon were planned. The actual control room where the lunar landings were monitored is still here, although today it is a national historic site and is no longer used. That room is also where controllers assisted the crew when part of the spaceship *Apollo 13* exploded thousands of miles from home. Because of good advice, helpful suggestions, hours of nerve-racking work, and a great deal of luck, the three men on that mission escaped death and made it safely back to Earth. But now, in the Mission Control Center that is used today, every shuttle flight is tracked; each link-up to the International Space Station is monitored.

Months and years of necessary preparation is done at Johnson. It is a vital location within the space industry today. There are things there that are not found elsewhere. The Mission Control Center itself, the vital heart of the enterprise, is a large place with rows and rows of computer terminals and huge maps and monitors across the front wall of the room. The rear of the room is glass, and behind that is a viewing gallery where interested spectators, media representatives, astronaut family members, and others come to watch ongoing space operations. Every second of every mission is monitored there.

In other buildings there are giant mock-ups of everything astronauts work with when they are in space. There they learn everything about the shuttles they ride and the space station they visit. All of these facilities have fancy names, but that does not detract from their purpose. One of these is the Space Environment Simulation Laboratory, where two very large vacuum chambers imitate the conditions that astronauts can expect in space. For instance, in the chambers temperatures can be elevated to 126 degrees Celcius, or lowered to as much as -173 degrees Celcius. There are exact models of the shuttles and their parts, the space station and its complexities, and the training room where pretend space walks can be practised.

The JSC has all kinds of simulators where the motion of a spaceship,

FASCINATING FACT
What Is the Neutral Buoyancy Laboratory?

It's the world's largest indoor swimming pool, where astronauts spend hours and hours training for space missions. The water area is longer and wider than the ice surface of a professional hockey rink, and is deep enough to cover a house. Astronauts use the pool to train because the weightlessness people experience when working underwater is like the weightlessness of working in space. Even though they're working in the water, the astronauts wear spacesuits. During these training periods, technicians in scuba gear are always close at hand in case of an emergency. The pool temperature is kept comfortably warm because the men and women who have to work submerged do so for hours at a time.

the roar of its launch, the view outside, and the pressure of added gravitational forces can be duplicated with amazing accuracy. Inside these large structures all kinds of pretend emergencies can be staged. These are usually so realistic that the astronaut-in-training leaves the simulator as exhausted as if he or she had been in a shuttle that was in trouble. After they have coped with all kinds of realistic emergencies, students develop the ability to react quickly to whatever problems they may encounter in space.

NASA photo

Canadian astronaut Dave Williams participates in underwater simulation of extravehicular activity (EVA) in the Neutral Buoyancy Laboratory, near the Johnson Space Center at Houston, Texas.

There is a large, exact-sized model of the space crane, or as it is known in Canada, the Canadarm. Astronauts use the model to learn how to operate the complex machine, which is used in space to complete tasks such as lifting satellites from the cargo bay to place them into a precise orbit. Operational training for the Canadarm involves hundreds of hours of careful, dedicated, and painstaking work. Several Canadian astronauts have become experts in its use.

Not all the training is done on machines. Long sessions are held in classrooms, where new students learn all kinds of subjects. Astronauts have to know a great deal about the Earth, the skies, the stars, the moon, and Mars. They have to know about the oceans, the winds, and what needs to happen if man wants to return to the moon and eventually travel beyond it. And because space travel is so international today, new astronauts often have to learn other languages — Russian being one of them — so they can work and live with astronauts from other countries. On the space station in particular, several languages are spoken, so there is a need to communicate effectively.

Another thing all astronauts have to know is how to remain healthy in space. They need to know how to handle space sickness, muscle loss, sleep difficulties, and lack of proper exercise. They have to recognize extreme fatigue, difficulty concentrating, and even learn how to cope with a headache or a cold. Preparation for flying means staying in shape. That is why astronauts spend hours in gymnasiums, on running tracks, and in the pool. They play several sports, including basketball, tennis, handball, squash, and sometimes even hockey. Because all of Canada's astronauts can fly planes and parachute, they spend hours training, practising, and working hard to be able to do these things proficiently.

Most astronauts will probably have a rather short career. One man went up in a shuttle when he was 77 years old, but the vast majority of astronauts do not remain active for that long. There are several reasons for this.

For one thing, most have other successful careers before they enter the space program. This has certainly been true for the Canadians. Some were doctors, one spent years in the navy, another flew fighter jets, some were scientists, one was an accomplished gymnast, another an underwater explorer. Such accomplishments took time to achieve, and all of our astronauts were slightly older when they were selected for space. Then, once they were in the program, they often had to wait a long time before actually getting a chance to fly.

The astronaut profession is highly competitive and often, after participants get one or more chances to fly, they begin to realize that few opportunities to do so lie ahead. That's why they often leave rather early, and return to work in the fields where they were first successful.

There are two other common reasons for stepping down. One is that being an astronaut is hard work, and it involves wear and tear on the human body that is unlike any other job. Men and women who have gone into space want to return to civilian life while they are healthy. The last, but extremely important, consideration is that home life is difficult for astronauts. Those in the program are often away from home. They sometimes see their loved ones only on rushed weekends, interrupted holidays, and stopovers between work-related world travels.

Yet, thousands and thousands of people want to become astronauts. They want to experience the thrill of a shuttle liftoff, the wonder of weightlessness, the pleasure of circling the Earth every 90 minutes, and the thrill of seeing the panorama of our planet from orbit. They want to walk in space, visit the space station, experience a de-orbit burn as the shuttle heads for home, and enjoy the pleasure of touchdown at the end of the journey.

As we know, several Canadians have made such trips. Certainly, they are lucky to have done so; they obviously have been well-qualified, and they are unique. But exactly who are they?

6 The First Canadian in Space

Marc Garneau was Canada's first astronaut. He flew in 1984, and went into space two more times after that. He performed well on each of his missions and became a national hero. His story is a magnificent one, and it shows the importance of hard work, determination, and luck.

When Marc was quite young he never dreamed of being an astronaut, because there was no such thing then. But when Yuri Gagarin flew, Garneau was 12, and he marvelled at the wonder of the event. Everyone he knew talked about this amazing thing that had happened in Russia. Then, just three weeks later, when the Americans launched *their* first manned spaceship, interest was even greater. By this time, young people knew that being an astronaut was the most exciting thing anyone could be. Boys everywhere wanted to fly in a spaceship. So did lots of girls. However, there was a problem.

Because he was a Canadian, Marc Garneau soon understood that he would likely never get to go into space. At first, only Russians and Americans were sent up in rockets. Marc had to put his hopes aside. He continued in school, all the while considering other occupations that appealed to him. Because his father was in the Canadian Army, Marc was familiar with life in uniform and what that involved, but while he knew a job as a soldier would be fulfilling, he didn't want to be just like his dad. Instead, he told his parents that he was going to join the

Canadian Navy. It might not be a career in space, but it offered opportunity, challenge, and a chance to see the world. He left Quebec City, where he was born and where he had received his early education, and enrolled at the Royal Military College in Kingston, Ontario. He got his first degree from there when he was 21, in engineering. Graduating from the Royal Military College meant he qualified as a naval officer, something that was a huge stepping stone in his career. The fact that he was fluently bilingual in French and English was also an asset.

Marc Garneau is a veteran of three space flights: STS-41G in 1984, STS-77 in 1996, and STS-97 in 2000.

Canadian Space Agency photo

Garneau always liked adventure and he looks back on his time in the navy as giving him plenty of that. He went to lots of new places, saw fascinating things, met interesting people, and increased his knowledge of the world. Because he always believed that in life he would use his brain as well as his body, he found the challenges that the navy offered attractive. After a time, he went to England and studied electrical engineering at the Imperial College of Science and Technology. This school is situated in London, one of the most fascinating cities in the world. Marc graduated from there with a Ph.D. degree. From them on he could be addressed as "Dr. Garneau," along with his rank in the navy. Two years before he became an astronaut, that rank was "commander," and it was earned after several navy assignments in Halifax, Ottawa, and elsewhere.

During the time that Commander Garneau was advancing in his navy career, other Canadians were working closely with an organization in the United States called the National Aeronautics and Space Administration, or NASA, to build a futuristic crane for a new spaceship the Americans were developing. The crane was a Canadian invention, and NASA needed it in order to lift cargo, or payloads, from the belly of a spaceship that would be called a shuttle. Because Canadians were able to construct the crane to the exact specifications needed, and because the device performed so well, United States officials suggested that one or more Canadians should be given the chance to accompany Americans into space. The invitation arrived in Ottawa, and many Canadian men, women, and even boys and girls answered it. In fact, nearly 4,400 people applied to become astronauts. One of them was Marc Garneau.

The competition lasted six months, and during that time Garneau and several other finalists for the job waited, worked, and hoped, until the six best-qualified individuals were told that they had been selected for astronaut training. Again, Garneau was among them. By this time he was 35 years old, married, and the father of twins named Yves and Simone. They were in elementary school, and while both were very proud of him, neither was quite sure what being a spaceman actually meant. However, before too long, they would find out.

At the same time that Marc Garneau was picked to do astronaut training, a young medical doctor working in Montreal was chosen as well. His name is Bob Thirsk. Soon the two men would become not only working partners and friends, but busier than they had ever been in their lives. This was because Garneau's first flight was only a few months away, and he had so much to do and learn before then. And, because Marc's "backup" was Dr. Thirsk, he too had to do the training — even though he didn't expect to fly himself. As backup, Thirsk's job was to be there, to train, and to be ready to go on the shuttle if anything happened to Garneau. Fortunately, nothing did. Much later, Bob Thirsk would get his opportunity to go into space as well.

FASCINATING FACT
What Does STS Mean?

These letters are short for "Space Transportation System." Each American space mission is numbered with STS and then a numeral. When Marc Garneau went on his first shuttle flight, the mission was referred to as STS-41G.

The two men worked in Ottawa for a brief time after their selection, but soon they reported to Houston to begin the rigorous, time-consuming, and non-stop weeks of preparation for Garneau's mission. He would blast off on the shuttle called *Challenger*, on a mission named STS-41G. Garneau's trip would be the sixth one that *Challenger* would make. At that time, two other shuttles were also being used: *Columbia* and *Discovery*.

There were several concerns that Garneau had to face in Houston. He had to be in the best possible condition physically, so he spent hours and hours running, swimming, and working out in the gym. He had to learn everything he could about the shuttle, how it worked, and the equipment it carried. Then he had to familiarize himself with the spacesuit he would wear. Its construction is highly technical — spacesuits are made according to specifications that are unbelievably complicated.

Garneau also had to understand several research experiments that Canadian scientists wanted him to do while he was in space. Every one of these was important, and the people who devised them wanted to get the best possible results. Marc was determined to do as well as he could. He knew that if he failed to do something correctly and completely the people relying on him back on Earth would be disappointed.

But getting to know as much as he could about the shuttle and how it worked was always on his mind. Garneau knew he would be flying with experienced astronauts, as well as beginners like himself, and he didn't want to look foolish in front of any of them, or be a burden to them. He realized that he likely would have to ask for help at times, but as the first Canadian in space, did not want to let his country down either.

Finally, as launch day grew near, Garneau and the rest of the crew left Houston and flew to the Kennedy Space Center. There, they were thrilled to see *Challenger* sitting on the launch pad, waiting for them. In Florida, they did media interviews, last minute training, checked pre-launch requirements, and had brief visits with family members. None of the crew were permitted time with their children though. This was because young people often pick up colds or other illnesses from classmates at school, and no astronaut is permitted to go into space if he or she is sick. In fact, years earlier, a man who had spent months training for a mission was grounded — because he had been exposed to German measles.

None of the men and women preparing to fly on STS-41G wanted *that* to happen.

Because all astronauts have to get ready for the journey ahead, they try to prepare themselves for it in every way possible. Marc's flight was scheduled to begin a few minutes after seven in the morning, but the preparation meant getting up in the middle of the night. For that reason, he and the others began going to bed earlier in the days immediately before departure. On launch day, they were wakened at three in the morning, because by the time they had showered, had a group breakfast, and had their spacesuits on, it was time to go to the launch pad.

Immediately outside the crew quarters, several reporters and photographers waited patiently for the astronauts to come out. When they did, the members of the media jostled for position, and the camera flashes seemed non-stop. The five crew men and two women smiled and waved as they walked in their spacesuits to a silver-coloured van that was parked nearby, its motor running. This vehicle is called the Astrovan. It's a medium-sized, camper-type bus that takes the astronauts to the launch pad. In less than two minutes they were all on board, and the driver had moved away. The trip is not long, only 15 kilometres or so, but it does take several minutes. Five or six police cars, their roof lights flashing, travel in front of and behind the little procession.

The day that Marc Garneau flew the morning air was cool and fresh as the Astrovan moved up the gradual slope to

Chris Hadfield and his fellow crew members walk out to the Astrovan that will take them to the shuttle. Hadfield is third from the right.

NASA photo

the launch pad. On all four sides, powerful search lights lit up the gleaming shuttle as it stood on its tail, poised and ready to go. As they climbed out of the van, the men and women who were about to fly glanced upwards and admired the great spaceship that stood before them. Then, with a hint of nervousness, they walked to an elevator that would whisk them up to what is called the white room, just outside the open hatch near the front of the shuttle. In that room, the astronauts are fitted with helmets, gloves, and communications gear before crawling into the spaceship.

Once inside, Garneau and the rest of the crew lay on their backs, their knees upward, as the specialists from the white room buckled them, one by one, into the seats they would use for the launch. When all seven fliers were on board and hooked up to the communications system, the hatch was closed and locked, and the moment of departure was at hand.

Later on, Marc Garneau admitted that he was somewhat fearful as the powerful engines of the spacecraft roared to life. But soon, amid the smoke, flame, and huge billowing clouds of steam, *Challenger* roared skyward and STS-41G began. Just over nine minutes later, the space-ship entered orbit, and Canada's first astronaut was circling the Earth. He was a happy man.

7 The First Canadian Woman in Space

Roberta Bondar was supposed to fly soon after Marc Garneau. However, that did not happen. In fact, more than seven years would pass before she became Canada's first female astronaut, and the second person from this country to go into space. The main reason for the delay was because of the loss of *Challenger*, the same shuttle that Garneau rode.

As we learned earlier in this book, the entire crew of the *Challenger* perished when it exploded above the Kennedy Space Center one very cold January morning in 1986. NASA didn't launch another shuttle until 1988.

Eventually, Roberta Bondar's hopes were realized when she flew at last. Her flight was the culmination of a lifelong dream for the young woman from Sault Ste. Marie, Ontario. She had been interested in space forever, it seemed, but the path from this planet was not easy for her. Despite excelling in school at every level, she often felt that succeeding as a female astronaut was especially hard, particularly in such a male-dominated profession. She was always interested in sports, science, and exploring, but far too often was told that these fields were for males only. Nevertheless, Roberta was determined to be the best she could be, and to go wherever her imagination and drive would take her. And, at long last, they took her to the mid-deck of the shuttle *Discovery* as it blasted from pad 39A at the Kennedy Space Center in Florida in January, 1992.

Family members and friends were there that day, but sadly, her father, who had always encouraged her to be whatever she could be, was not. Edward Bondar had died of a heart attack shortly before the *Challenger* loss. No doubt he would have been especially proud of Roberta when she flew. Everyone in her hometown certainly was, and the news of the launch was the main topic of conversation everywhere groups gathered. Individuals bragged because they knew Roberta, had gone to school with her, or simply because they had seen her in a

local store a couple of years earlier. It was indeed an important day for the northwestern Ontario town on the American border.

And it was a special day for her sister, Barbara. Barbara was well aware of the difficulties Roberta had overcome in the years that led up to that day. She knew her younger sister had always been a top student in elementary school, high school, and university. She knew Roberta had been named female athlete of the year at Sir James Dunn Collegiate in Sault Ste. Marie, and she knew of the many university degrees her sister had earned. She also knew that Roberta was a scuba diver, an airplane pilot, a scientist and a medical doctor. And she knew that this Canadian would be as much of a success in space as she had been on the ground.

Roberta Bondar is a veteran of one space flight: STS-42 in 1992.

Canadian Space Agency photo

Apart from a short delay because of weather, the launch countdown proceeded smoothly on that final day. There had been many postponements earlier.

As always, the shuttle crew relied on the computers that were a vital part of the launch sequence. Finally, the long-anticipated countdown concluded, and *Discovery* was airborne. Inside it, the seven astronauts remained on their backs as the great ship roared higher and higher, until the straps that held them in their seats suddenly eased, their helmets were no longer heavy, and the gravitational pull of the Earth was no more.

Space at last!

That was when each astronaut took off the bulky, cumbersome, but necessary, launch and entry suits and helmets they wore. For the rest of the time in space, they wore casual clothes, often T-shirts, shorts, and socks, because these provided comfort in the working environment on board. The seats used for launch were taken down and stored. They would not be needed again until the final part of the mission, when the shuttle was about to return to Earth. Already, the most obvious joys of being in space were noted in fun ways. A pen used to make notes floated away from the individual using it. And so did his memo pad when the astronaut tried to grab for the pen.

But it was what could be seen from the shuttle windows that enthralled everyone. On the flight deck there is a wraparound view of the Earth and space that is said to be breathtaking. There the astronauts can see the greens, golds, and browns of the continents in all their magnificence; the vast and varied blues of the oceans; the clouds that drift across the sky; and the deep, limitless, velvet blackness of space. Even crew members who had been in space before and seen the view already were in awe of what was before them. But the rookies on board, who had never seen such things, were excited. They were laughing, talking, shrieking, and pointing — all at the same time. *This*, they told themselves, made all the years of work, worry, postponement, and persistence worthwhile. They were seeing the Earth from space — a wondrous spectacle that few human beings have seen or will ever see.

Of necessity, the sightseeing soon came to an end. This voyage of *Discovery* was not a long one, and every minute of every hour had to be used completely. No matter how wonderful the view might be there was lots of work to be done, and time for sightseeing was limited. On that mission, for the first time, there was a place to work that was totally unique. That place was really a thing, called Spacelab, a laboratory that rested in the shuttle payload bay.

On previous shuttle flights, scheduled experiments, scientific work, crew testing, and so on had to be done on either the flight deck or mid-deck of the spaceship. Now, with Spacelab on board, Roberta Bondar and the other scientists on the flight had their own facility that provided more room, a unique environment, and a location where several complex studies could be done.

The lab working conditions were ideal, although noisy because of fans and other electrical equipment that was constantly humming. For the most part though, the scientists learned to tune out the racket and concentrate on their work. They wore headsets when communicating with scientists on the ground, who offered advice and encouragement when the various experiments were being done. At night, crew members often wore earplugs to deaden the sound so they could sleep.

On this flight a whole array of living organisms were passengers. These included frog eggs, mouse cells, stick insects, and fruit flies. On later flights, mice have been brought on board and dissected in space. The creatures that were on this mission were studied for various reasons, one of them was to learn how other species would adapt to space. Roberta Bondar was quite involved in the experiments. Roberta and her crewmates also participated in several experiments designed to further understanding of how the human body performs in the absence of gravity. Two of the changes the body undergoes are of particular interest. Both happened to Roberta.

On Earth, she wears glasses for some of her work. In space, however, she not only didn't need her glasses at all, she misplaced them and they floated away, disappearing somewhere in the spaceship. Fortunately, she did locate them before she was back on Earth — where she would need them again.

FASCINATING FACT
What Is a Spacelab?

A Spacelab is a scientific laboratory which can fit inside a space shuttle cargo bay. The lab is a large, round cylinder almost 4 metres in diameter and 5 metres long. During the flight, all seven astronauts were inside it for some of the work, and for a group photo. The entry was through a tunnel from the mid-deck, and crew members leaving and entering floated through this tunnel.

The other change that Roberta noticed happened not only to her, but to the rest of the crew. In space she became taller! This is because without gravity, there is nothing to pull the human spine downward. As a result, most astronauts are an inch or so taller in space than they are on Earth. Roberta said later that for the first time in her life she was taller than her sister, Barbara. However, shortly after returning to Earth, she "shrank" to her normal size.

On this flight, as on others, a large IMAX camera was on board to document the journey. Back on Earth, the pictures produced would be shown in specially equipped theatres, where the screen is extremely large. You may have been to an IMAX movie, but if you haven't, try to go to one. You will not be in space, of course, but viewing the pictures on the big screen will help you appreciate the views of the Earth and sky that astronauts are lucky enough to see.

Roberta also participated in some of the press conferences that were held. She and the other crew members answered questions from reporters, officials involved in the space programs in various countries, school children, and politicians — one of them was the president of the United States. A couple of days later the Canadian prime minister called too. His name was Brian Mulroney, and he praised Roberta for the work she was doing, and told her that all of Canada was proud of her. Part of the conversation was in English, part in French. Before it concluded, Roberta Bondar told the prime minister that it was a great honour to represent her country in space.

Midway through the mission, the astronauts on *Discovery* were thrilled when Houston told them that their flight would last for eight days, not the seven that had been scheduled earlier. The extra hours meant that they had more time to spend on their experiments: monitoring the changes to the human body in space, studying how humans can judge what is "up" and what is "down" when there is no gravitational resistance, and exploring why astronauts returning from space often feel tired, dizzy, or faint.

But all too soon, in spite of the extra day in orbit, the mission came to an end.

The seats for the return to Earth were put back in place, the astronauts put on their launch and entry suits, and Mission Control in Houston gave permission to land. At the end of the flight, *Discovery* touched down at Edwards Air Force Base in California. The landing was a good one. For those on the shuttle that day, the memories of eight wonderful days in space would never fade.

# 8 Life on a Space Shuttle

Despite the fact that most of us have seen television coverage of launches and news conferences broadcast from shuttles, we know little about day-to-day life on a spaceship. That's too bad, because what astronauts do as they whiz around the globe is interesting and well worth examining. And it is certainly much different than daily life on Earth. This is particularly true because of the absence of gravity.

No matter whether astronauts are exercising, working, eating, sleeping, or even going to the bathroom, the lack of gravity determines the way they must act. It also has a role in how things around them are handled. They just can't set a wristwatch down and expect it to stay in the same place; it would just float away. So will anything else: a comb, a pen, a toothbrush. Just getting used to being in space requires lots of adjustment. Some of this begins on Earth, during the training period. Astronauts first experience reduced gravity in a special kind of airplane — an airplane with a decidedly unpleasant nickname.

It is called a vomit comet!

Without gravity, blood that normally flows to the legs and feet shifts to the upper body. Once that happens, shuttle crew members notice that their faces become puffy, that they often get headaches, and that they sometimes feel extremely tired and nauseous. In fact, most astronauts

FASCINATING FACT
What Is the "Vomit Comet?"

A specially equipped airplane in which astronauts train. The pilot flies higher and higher and then takes the plane into a steep dive. This manoeuvre is sort of like going over the top on a Ferris wheel or roller coaster. When this happens, the astronauts in the back become weightless for up to half a minute, allowing them to float around and get a taste of what it's like to be in space. The walls are padded so they won't injure themselves. Unfortunately, when the plane goes into a dive, they sometimes throw up!

During these flights, the pilots have their seatbelts firmly buckled of course. They have to fly the plane!

endure stomach discomfort, and some throw up. Fortunately, there are now medications that help prevent this.

Scientists know that because the inner ear, the organ of balance, is confused by the lack of gravity, attempts to adapt to weightlessness often make people feel ill. The technical term is Space Adaptation Syndrome, although it is commonly referred to as space sickness. For most men and women on orbit, the discomfort generally disappears after a couple of days. Strangely, the problem rarely occurs after someone's first flight. It is as if the body "remembers" how to adapt to weightlessness and does. This means that the misery of being sick is mainly a problem for first-time fliers.

But on their first flight, astronauts have to learn how to move around inside a spaceship. There is always a temptation to move too quickly from one location to another. That usually results in bumping into walls, simply because there is nothing to slow movement. Writing about this experience, one astronaut said that he finally realized he could "push off" from one place to another with little more than the movement of one finger.

During the times they are working, astronauts use foot restraints so that they can remain in position and not float away from their work. Of course, in space there is no "up" or "down" so some individuals prefer to work "upside down." At first, this might seem both unusual and bothersome, but not for long. After a few hours on orbit, body position becomes less and less important.

What is important, however, is the proper placement of equipment used for work, or things needed for daily living. For that reason, Velcro is particularly useful. If an astronaut has to check information for a shuttle function, the instruction manual can be kept close at hand by pressing it to a Velcro strip on the wall. So can a microphone, a clipboard, a camera, or most other items that must be kept close at hand. Often, the Velcro strips are colour-coded for easy and quick identification.

As might be expected, eating and drinking in space involves ever-evolving adaptation. Most of the meal preparation for a flight is done on Earth, often long before the spaceship leaves the launch pad. In the weeks leading up to a mission, the astronauts make their food preferences known to the dieticians and food scientists whose job is to ensure nutritious and balanced in-flight meals. Any food allergies are taken into account, and favourite treats are allowed. Fresh fruits, such as apples or bananas, are packed shortly before takeoff.

In contrast to what was offered in the early days of space travel, a vast variety of foods are available today. Astronauts used to only get cold, unappetizing, bland food. Now, space food is good enough that few astronauts complain about it. There is lots of choice, and improvements are always being made. Good food is important on short missions, but an absolute necessity on the International Space Station, where men and women spend months on orbit.

But even at the space station, the food is generally better than one might think. This is partly because fresh supplies are brought each time a spacecraft visits. Included in the deliveries are a variety of foods, but some are avoided because of problems they might cause — cake, for example, could crumble and float. So could pizza or breakfast cereal. No one would ever attempt to pour Cheerios or Rice Krispies into a bowl in space. For one thing, they wouldn't fall into the bowl; they would fly all over the place, and the bowl would float away too.

The crew members often play with their fruit juices, particularly first-time flyers. The tiniest bit of orange juice poured out of a container remains suspended and forms a globule. It is always fun to retrieve the floating juice by sucking it up with a drinking straw.

On board, food can be heated in a small convection oven, but there are no refrigerators for leftovers on any of the shuttles, because they would take up too much room. Many meals are eaten with a spoon because whatever the ingredient, it sticks to a spoon. Most space food is freeze-dried and kept available in plastic pouches. At meal time, the contents are prepared by penetrating the pouch with a blunt needle and adding hot or cold water. Then the pouch is massaged until the contents are moist and tasty.

The toilet on a space shuttle is unlike a toilet on Earth. For one thing, the person using it must be strapped in place.

John Melady photo

Brushing one's teeth, using the toilet, and washing all present particular challenges. Often, astronauts simply swallow the toothpaste they have used, or spit it into a facecloth. There is no sink with running water to rinse one's mouth. And showers are not really showers as we know them on Earth. In fact, they are really not showers at all. The astronauts enter an enclosed cubicle and clean up with a sponge bath. Hot water, a moist cloth, and rinseless soap are used.

During all flights, astronauts must exercise in order to stay in shape. If they don't their bones and muscles weaken, and after landing they might not be able to walk off the shuttle. In fact, even when they have worked out regularly during a flight, some individuals still find it difficult to move with confidence when they first return to Earth. A few have even fainted. Fortunately, they regain their strength quite quickly and are generally able to carry on with their regular duties.

In space, shuttle crew members can move without much effort, so they don't need to exert themselves very much. The lack of exertion and the absence of gravity cause muscles to deteriorate. Exercise prevents at least some of this from happening.

There are several ways of keeping in shape, and a number of machines that can be used to help. Over time, shuttles have had modified exercise bikes on board, rowing machines, treadmills, and other devices, but all have to be operated differently from the way they would be used on Earth. For example, in order to keep from floating away from an exercise bike a kind of cloth seatbelt is used to ensure that the rider remains on the bike. He or she also has to remember to clip their shoes to the pedals before starting the workout.

Sleeping on board a spaceship is not exactly like sleeping at home. Some astronauts say they would rather sleep in space than on Earth, they find they get a very restful sleep as they whirl around the globe. On the shuttles, sleeping compartments are situated along the starboard (right) wall of the mid-deck. Astronauts use

FASCINATING FACT
How Do You Use the Toilet in Space?

When using the toilet, each astronaut must secure him or herself in place with thigh restraints. If they didn't, they'd float away from the seat. Solid and liquid waste are separated and sucked into a storage container by fans. The contents are disinfected and removed later. The movements required to use the toilet on the shuttle are practised on Earth long before the flight leaves the ground.

Astronaut Bjarni Tryggvason sleeping during a shuttle flight. Note that his arms are floating because of the absence of gravity.

NASA photo

sleeping bags, as if they were on a camping trip. A sliding panel provides some privacy and shuts out the light and noise. Each compartment has a light and a fresh-air vent. Because of the lack of gravity, the astronauts generally strap themselves down with sleep restraints. If they didn't, they might find themselves floating out in the crew area if they forget to close the sliding panel when they go to bed.

There is a story about an astronaut who fell asleep as he sat using his laptop. He ended up drifting across the deck with his arms and legs in the fetal position. He even continued snoring as other crew members laughingly pushed him back to where he should have been. Later on, he didn't remember any of his floating adventure.

All of the men and women who go into space treasure the experience. It is unique, unforgettable, and something few get a chance to do. And even though travelling on a shuttle, or living for months on the International Space Station is confining, at times lonely, and always dangerous, it is the adventure of a lifetime for those who get to do it.

The Space Vision System

Marc Garneau and Roberta Bondar were the first Canadians in space. However, there are many other Canadian astronauts whose flights were just as exciting. One of them is Steve MacLean, a slim, athletic man who was born and raised in Ottawa. While he did lots of things of interest before he became as astronaut, it was his skills as a gymnast that drew attention to him. In fact, MacLean was so good in the sport that he was on Canada's national team for three years. He also goes on long hikes to unusual places. On one of these adventures he walked to the base of Mount Everest, the highest mountain in the world.

Steve's father was a scientist, and he always hoped his son would follow in his footsteps. And Steve did — in part. He always liked science in school and he was good in that subject. That was why his parents were not surprised when, after finishing elementary and secondary school, their son told them he wanted to take science at university. But he didn't want to stay in Ottawa, he wanted to go to school in Toronto, at York University. Steve did well there, and after he earned a doctorate in physics from York he went on to do further studies in California.

One day, while he was living in the United States, MacLean received a letter from a friend, telling him that Canada was about to enter the space program. Young Canadian men and women would be chosen to be astronauts. Steve's friend thought he might be interested in the job. He was. He applied right away, and was chosen.

One of the other Canadians selected for the space program was Bjarni Tryggvason, who happened to be working in MacLean's hometown, Ottawa, at the time. The two were soon in Houston, and after months of training together, Steve got his first chance to fly on the shuttle *Columbia*, in mission STS-52. Bjarni was his backup.

On that flight, Steve MacLean had several jobs to do, but the most important of all was to test what was called the Space Vision System (**SVS**). The SVS was a kind of sophisticated television facility designed to direct the Canadarm in space. Both the arm and the Vision System were Canadian inventions, and Steve wanted to make sure they worked perfectly together, so that whenever an astronaut used the Canadarm it moved to the exact location desired, and performed the precise function its operator intended.

The SVS had not been tested in space before Steve's first flight. He was well aware that a lot was depending on his expertise, so he worked very hard to make sure that the new closed-circuit television system functioned perfectly. Fortunately, it did.

Of course, Canada's third astronaut to reach space had many other duties on the mission. He helped launch an Italian satellite. He used something called a Sun Photo Spectrometer to measure the ozone and other gases that exist in outer parts of the Earth's atmosphere. The ozone layer helps protect the Earth

FASCINATING FACT
What Is the Canadarm?

The Canadarm is a big space crane built in Canada. It is both unique and necessary on every one of the space shuttles. The Americans often call it the Remote Manipulator System, but to Canadians the machine is the Canadarm. In the years since it was first built, the arm has been modified a number of times, extended, and in a somewhat different version, installed on the International Space Station. But in all forms, and in all locations, the invention itself is truly unique. Sometimes it is called a space crane, because it is used to lift heavy objects in space.

The arm is 15 metres long and works very much like a giant human arm. It has a shoulder, an elbow, a wrist, and even a kind of hand capable of grasping all sorts of things, especially payloads being carried in the shuttle cargo compartment. The base of the arm is located within this cargo bay. The Canadarm is so strong that in space it can lift almost 30,000 kilograms (66,000 pounds), but on Earth, because of gravity, it cannot support itself. For that reason, testing the machine was difficult. Refinements to the design were made using a kind of moveable cradle on a large, flat factory floor. Despite all the problems associated with building and perfecting the arm, it worked as intended in space and has been flying successfully for 30 years.

from the harmful ultraviolet rays of the sun. Steve also took photographs to try to determine why a space shuttle emits a glow on one side of its surface while in orbit. The photos were intended to help scientists solve the mystery of the glow, which was something like the aurora borealis, or northern lights.

Steve also used a tiny furnace to melt metals so that scientists on Earth could figure out how particular metals mixed without gravity, and when exposed to extremely high temperatures. The idea was that by melding molten metal, new, stronger, and more useful materials might be discovered. Another experiment Steve MacLean did was to expose certain materials to the harshness of space, so that their durability could be better understood. This experiment involved plastic and other such substances.

But the Space Vision System was what held his closest attention, and involved the most precise work imaginable. The SVS was tested near the end of the flight, so that possible shuttle vibration during earlier experiments would not interfere with the workings of the new invention when it was still under study.

Fortunately, the SVS worked well. Steve used it to move a mini satellite in the shuttle's cargo bay. He gave the task his entire concentration, and ever so slowly and carefully achieved what he wanted. In fact, he worked so hard at what he was doing that the shuttle commander offered to have other crew members assist. However, the main task was Steve's alone, and when his work was completed, he was satisfied with the results. So was Bjarni Tryggvason, back on Earth. The two had helped design the SVS and Tryggvason followed every move MacLean made. In fact, as backup, he would have been able to make the same manoeuvres had Steve taken ill, or for some reason had not been able to fly.

During the mission, *Columbia* passed over an area of the South Pacific Ocean where a 20-metre-long canoe was sailing for hundreds of miles from what was known as the Cook Islands to the American state of Hawaii. The long voyage was meant to retrace the same route that men and women had followed in ancient times. Those ancient travellers were explorers, and now the crew of the spaceship were explorers too.

In order to compare to the two journeys, a radio connection was made between the groups. Everyone marvelled at how different their methods of travel were. Down on the surface of the

Veteran astronaut and Canadian mission specialist, Steve MacLean. Dr. MacLean is now president of the Canadian Space Agency. His term in office began in 2008.

NASA photo

sea, the canoe moved slowly, drifting with the winds and the waves. High above, the great spaceship zipped around the globe every 90 minutes or so. But the sailors and the astronauts were all on journeys of discovery.

As the two groups of explorers talked, they were linked by satellite to school children in Hawaii. The students wanted to know all about the two methods of travel, and they had good questions for both crews. One boy asked Steve MacLean how he kept in shape in space. As the young people in Hawaii watched on a television screen, MacLean demonstrated his answer. He moved to the centre of the mid-deck and did several floating sit-ups. The audience on Earth cheered. Most were not aware that Steve was a former champion gymnast, even though the sit-ups might not have been as good as they once were. However, the young people all thought the performance was quite wonderful. As they sat on the floor of the school gymnasium, several tried to do what Steve did. Most failed though, and realized that you had to be in good shape to do several of the exercises in a row.

Soon after the SVS tests were complete it was time for *Columbia* to head for home. As always, everything on the shuttle had to

FASCINATING FACT
Landing Space Shuttles

If possible, returning space shuttles land at the Kennedy Space Center. When there are problems with the weather in Florida, they land at Edwards Air Force Base in California. If, for some reason, both of these locations are not suitable, landings can be made at White Sands, New Mexico.

FASCINATING FACT
Runways for Shuttle Landings

The main runway at the Kennedy Space Center in Florida is 4,572 metres long and just over 91 metres wide. The one at Edwards Air Force Base in California is the same. These dimensions are roughly twice as long and twice as wide as most commercial airport runways.

be stowed and secured before the craft screamed through the atmosphere on its return to our planet. The seats on the flight deck and mid-deck were put back in place, the astronauts got into their launch and entry suits again, and *Columbia* raced toward Earth. As it did so, the contact with the atmosphere of Earth engulfed the shuttle in the thousands of degrees of flame and fire that the crew could see on every side. This wild ride during the approach to our planet is always one that astronauts remember, often with a bit of nervousness, and they feel thankful they are shielded from the inferno outside. Fortunately, the return was a safe one.

In all, Steve MacLean and his shipmates had been away for only 10 days. But those 10 days had been part of a marvelous journey. *Columbia* had spun around the world a total of 159 times. Still, for Steve and everyone else on board, seeing family members again was just as wonderful as their trip.

The shuttle touched down on Runway 33 at the Kennedy Space Center, and soon after the returning astronauts got a chance to hug their loved ones. But the reunion was brief. The travellers were whisked away for examinations by the medical staff at KSC. Even though all of the astronauts appeared to be in good health, the doctors wanted to be sure. They also wanted to learn how being in space affected each crew member. But soon each flier was allowed to rejoin his or her family, and tell them about their adventure. Later, Steve MacLean would return to space, but just then he was happy to be back on Earth. And his wife, Nadine, and their children, Jean-Phillipe and Catherine, were *really* glad to have Dad home again.

A Canadian Visits *Mir*

A short distance outside the city of Sarnia, Ontario, is a small airport. It has excellent runways, a modern passenger terminal, and plenty of parking. The place is rarely busy, so if you happen to be there sometime, have a look around. There is not much to see, but a particular photo on the wall always gets attention.

The photograph is of an F-18 aircraft and a Canadian Air Force pilot who is identified in the caption below the picture. The kind of jet in the photo is currently Canada's most sophisticated fighter plane, and anyone who has attended an air show has likely seen it. It is sleek, fast, and futuristic, and those who fly it are highly skilled, and oh so cool! The man in the picture certainly is. His name is Chris Hadfield — and he was born in Sarnia.

In fact, the airport is named after him.

But Chris Hadfield is much more than a fighter pilot. He is one of the best fighter pilots around, and a few years ago he was *the* best. That was when this soft-spoken young Canadian was named the top test pilot in the United States Navy. Before that, he had gone to the States and flown against the most skilled pilots there. After a lot of practice, demonstration flying, and aerial competitions, in 1991 it was determined that Chris Hadfield was the best pilot of all. It was an unforgettable achievement for Chris, who grew up on a corn farm just outside the town of Milton, Ontario, where the family moved when he was a boy. His father, Roger, who had flown for many years with Air Canada, was especially proud of his son, who had inherited his love for flying and was obviously very good at it.

Not long after, in 1995, Roger and Eleanor Hadfield were able to marvel at their son's success in another type of flying. That was when Chris flew from Cape Canaveral, Florida, as an astronaut on the space shuttle *Atlantis*. He was a mission specialist on STS-74, and the first and only Canadian to visit the Russian space station *Mir*, which had been circling the Earth for some time. Six years later, in 2001, it was determined that *Mir* had come to the end of its useful life, and it was abandoned. Eventually, it drifted closer to Earth and burned up in the atmosphere over the Pacific Ocean. Chris was always glad that he had had the chance to visit there while it was still in operation.

FASCINATING FACT
The Beginning of a Dream

When Chris Hadfield was nine years old, he watched the first moon landing on television. The television images of Neil Armstrong stepping onto the moon amazed young Chris so much that he decided that when he grew up, he would become an astronaut. Many years later, he did just that.

While Chris Hadfield didn't become an astronaut overnight, he had dreamed of being one from the time he was nine. When he became a teenager, then an adult, the dreams never died. In fact, they became more pressing as the years passed.

Chris knew in his own mind that the chances of fulfilling his wish might be greater if he joined the air force and became a jet pilot. Along the way, he finished school, got high marks, and learned to fly a glider before he was old enough to drive a car. When he was 16 he qualified on power planes as well.

Chris Hadfield has always been athletic and he is interested in several activities. He enjoys running, horseback riding, and playing squash and volleyball, but his favourite sport when he was in high school was skiing. He loved the speed and the thrill of careening down a hill as fast as he could. He even taught ski racing for a while. In his spare time he sings, plays the guitar, and writes. In essence, he is what could be called an all-round achiever. Chris is married, the father of three grown children, and they, like their parents, are all achievers. His wife,

Helene, whom he calls the most important person in his life, rides horses, and was his girlfriend in high school. They have been a devoted couple for many years.

Chris excelled at university, and obtained degrees both in Canada and in the United States. However, he was always most at home as the pilot of a plane — any plane. To date, he has flown over 70 different types, from the tiniest and slowest to the fastest and most sophisticated. In fact, some of the jets he test flew were down-right dangerous, and many of his friends were killed flying them. Those tragedies all affected Chris, but he never stopped pursuing his dreams. As soon as he learned that Canada was going to hire astronauts, he applied. Since then, he has never looked back.

The crew of STS-74 pose in front of Atlantis *after their return to Earth. Chris Hadfield is on the left.*

NASA photo

There are four main groups of astronauts who ride the American space shuttles. The commanders and pilots fly them. Payload specialists are crew members who go into space in order to work on scientific experiments; their main focus is on the studies they do during the flight. The Canadians who flew first — Marc Garneau, Roberta Bondar, and Steve MacLean — were all payload specialists. Later, both Garneau and MacLean upgraded their qualifications and became mission specialists, making them better trained and giving them a greater overall knowledge of the shuttles and how they operated. Chris Hadfield was Canada's first mission specialist in orbit, but he and Marc Garneau trained together in order to qualify themselves.

The *Atlantis*, carrying Hadfield and his fellow crew members, blasted off at 9:30 in the morning on November 12. The day was rather cold by Florida standards, but in spite of the temperature, safety conditions were acceptable and the liftoff went ahead as scheduled. This was important because that day there was just a 10 minute time slot when liftoff could occur. This brief period, or "window," as it is referred to in space technology, was significant because the shuttle was being sent to link-up with *Mir*, then in its own orbit high above the Earth. If *Atlantis* did not go when it was supposed to go, it would not have been able to catch Mir until a later time. If that happened, the mission wouldn't be completed under the best possible circumstances.

As always happens with early shuttle departures, the astronauts were wakened in the middle of the night. By sunrise they were in the silver Astrovan, en route to the spaceship. They had already showered, had breakfast together, and were dressed in their orange launch and entry suits. For the most part, the short drive to the pad was a quiet one. There was some friendly banter, but even the natural jokesters were rather subdued. Being strapped into a tiny chamber, on top of a mighty rocket, is exciting but also sobering. Unless the thousands of operations that lead to every launch all work, properly and in sequence, there is always the danger that something could go wrong. Going up in a spaceship is one of the most dangerous ventures imaginable. Some say it is like sitting on a bomb that could explode at any minute.

Chris Hadfield remembers being strapped into his shuttle seat that morning. He remembers the good wishes of the technicians who assisted. He remembers being hooked up to

FASCINATING FACT
What Was *Mir*?

Mir was a Russian space station, launched in 1986. In English, the Russian word *mir* means "peace." The station was in orbit for 15 years. During that time, many scientific experiments were done there, all with the aim of developing technology that will let humans live in space permanently. The station was the predecessor of the International Space Station, which is currently in orbit. Chris Hadfield was its only Canadian visitor. *Mir* was eventually abandoned and it fell out of orbit on March 21, 2001.

the intercom and the long, nervous wait before departure. During that time, as they lay on their backs, their knees up, ready for launch, he and the rest of the crew had plenty of time to think. They had said goodbye to their loved ones the night before, they had done all the training possible, and they were as prepared as they ever would be for the most exciting adventure of their lives — as long as everything worked properly.

The countdown continued.

In those last seconds before launch, the public address announcer's voice boomed over the Kennedy compound. "Ten, nine, eight, seven," he counted. The thousands of spectators listened, held their breath, and waited for "zero," and "liftoff!" When these words were said, all eyes focused on the pad and the mighty machine on it. For a couple of seconds there was neither noise nor motion — as if the shuttle did not want to move.

But then towering steam and smoke clouds billowed from the flame trench under the rocket as the white-hot fire from millions of litres of fuel ripped the spaceship from its moorings, sending it arching to the heavens. The booming roar of the engines actually shook the ground. Up on the roof of the Launch Control Center, the astronauts' family members huddled and hoped for a safe journey for their loved ones. Helene Hadfield was there among them.

On the decks of *Atlantis*, the astronauts remained strapped in their seats as the mighty vehicle pitched, shook, and shot to the sky. Feelings of apprehension bordering on fear gave way to smiles of relief. Already, the ship was in contact with Houston, where Mission Control would handle all communications for the rest of the journey. Outside, the solid rocket boosters and the massive orange external tank were jettisoned. In what seemed like no time, the ship was in orbit. The pull of gravity disappeared and the men in the spacesuits were now spacemen. One of them was Chris Hadfield. His long-held dreams had come true at last. Today, he remembers the happiness he felt then. *Atlantis* was in orbit, gravity was gone, and the beautiful blue-green Earth was far below.

Quickly, as on every flight, the seats the astronauts had been using were taken down and stowed, their launch suits were replaced with casual attire, and the rest of the gear needed during liftoff was tucked away. No one wanted it floating through the cabin during the mission. Once those chores were completed, every crew member rushed to the windows to check the view.

The author with veteran Canadian astronaut Chris Hadfield, at Cape Canaveral.

John Melady photo

Memories of the incredible scenery would remain with each for the rest of their lives. The problem would be describing it for family members and others who would ask: "What's it like in space?" To those on board, every answer they would give would be inadequate. The experience was just too awesome to describe.

But there was work to be done.

The main focus of STS-74 was the transport of what was called a docking module to *Mir*. The module was a kind of tunnel that would be attached to the Russian station so that supplies could be offloaded from *Atlantis*. Hundreds of kilograms of food, water, and scientific equipment would all be passed through the module and left on *Mir*. However, before any offloading could be done, *Atlantis* had to travel thousands and thousands of miles through the blackness of space, find *Mir*, and complete the dangerous and challenging link-up with the station. These operations tested the abilities of the pilots and the particular skills of others on board, including the Canadian mission specialist on his first flight. In fact, Chris Hadfield had a vital role to play once the shuttle was docked with *Mir*. He had to operate the Canadarm and lift the tunnel out of the shuttle cargo bay so that the module could be attached to *Mir*. In doing so, he would be the first Canadian to use the Canadarm in space. His role would be critical, his job difficult, and his accomplishment historic.

Fortunately, he performed exactly as required, and precisely as trained.

The new tunnel was bolted onto *Mir*. The connecting hatches between the shuttle and the station were opened, and the crew members from *Atlantis* were able to float freely into the Russian spaceship. The three men who had been living there for the previous three months were delighted to have visitors. Chris Hadfield was just as delighted to see them and visit their home in the sky.

The two spaceships remained locked together until all the supplies had been transferred and a few other requirements had been met. Then the crews gave each other bear hugs, handshakes, and high fives, and *Atlantis* prepared to depart. On the way back to Earth, Chris Hadfield was already starting to hope that he might return to space in the future. He was now sure his dreams would allow for that.

Hockey Shot in Space

In the spring of 1996, within a short period of time, two Canadians were launched on shuttles from Cape Canaveral. On May 19, Marc Garneau left for a 10-day mission on the space-ship *Endeavour*. His flight was called STS-77. A month later, astronaut Bob Thirsk began a 16-day trip on *Columbia*. His flight was STS-78. Both were successful and safe. Marc travelled four million miles, Bob about seven million. The two journeys ended on Runway 33 at the Kennedy Space Center.

Even though Marc Garneau had been in space once already, he was as excited about his second flight as he had been about the earlier one. Almost 12 years had passed since he first flew, and in that time he had travelled from coast to coast in Canada and to many other countries as well. On those trips he often visited schools and talked to students. There are hundreds of individuals across the country who remember Canada's first astronaut coming into their classroom, speaking about space, answering questions, and signing autographs for anyone who asked. On those visits he usually wore a flight suit, which certainly set him apart from those around him. He *looked* like an astronaut, and that fact, as well as what he said, helped his audiences remember him. He was friendly, helpful, and always encouraging.

MAPLE LEAF IN SPACE

Marc Garneau became so well-known that lots of things have been named after him — everything from roads, to parks, to schools. One of them is Marc Garneau Collegiate in Toronto. The students who go there have always been proud that their school was named after an astronaut. In the years since the collegiate got its name, Marc has visited several times, and some class members and teachers have even gone to Cape Canaveral to watch shuttle launches.

Because Bob Thirsk was backup for Garneau's first flight, he knew Marc well and often travelled to schools, town halls, and public auditoriums with Canada's first astronaut. In fact, Bob used to say he went along to help Marc carry his suitcases, because the first spaceman was too busy to do so. He was always signing autographs for people who came to meet him and hear him speak. Bob Thirsk also made many speeches about being an astronaut, but he knew that until he flew himself he would never really understand the joy, excitement, and danger of going into space. No wonder he was glad that right after Marc's second mission he also found himself in a shuttle, waiting for the countdown at Cape Canaveral. Finally, Bob understood how wondrous space travel was. As he soared into the heavens and entered orbit he was happy beyond words.

Just imagine doing what these brave men did! Think of how thrilled you would be to do the same thing. And, yes, even though you might be quite nervous, you would be really excited. Who knows, someday you might go into space yourself, just as Marc Garneau and Bob Thirsk did.

But what did they do on their missions?

They did many things — for science, for this country, for the world. Both men learned a lot. They adapted to living where gravity was almost non-existent; where they could float unhindered inside the shuttles they rode and move with little more than the touch of a finger. They learned to eat from sealed packages, where spilled orange juice would become a round, floating ball and remain suspended, where eating could be done in an "upside down" position, where sleeping was like floating on a cloud.

In the years between his flights, and when he was not travelling elsewhere, Marc Garneau trained rigorously at the Johnson Space Center in Texas. He was a payload specialist when he was in space the first time, a mission specialist on the second. In the mission specialist role he had more responsibility for the overall shuttle operation. He also knew more about how things worked than on his first flight. Back then he sometimes joked that he had just gone

FASCINATING FACT
Life Without Gravity

In space, there is really no "up" or "down" because there is no gravity. Astronauts do not have to have their feet on the floor of the shuttle in order to do their work. They can get things done just as easily if their feet are toward the ceiling.

along for the ride. And while that was not really the case, on his second mission he had more important duties. He operated the Canadarm. On the flight a gold-covered boxlike satellite, called Spartan, was placed in orbit by another mission specialist. Later, it was retrieved and gently brought back on board by Marc. The Spartan was a research tool for astronomers, who study objects beyond the atmosphere of Earth.

There were also some Canadian experiments that Marc helped complete. These were done inside a large scientific laboratory that rested in the cargo bay. There, astronauts had extra room to do the testing and observation each experiment demanded. Part of the work was observing baby fish, which were carried in a large plastic container. Scientists on Earth wanted to know how these tiny creatures would move from place to place when there was no gravity. The astronauts did the study, which helped scientists understand how fish navigate from one feeding area to another in the oceans.

There were also two experiments for students back on Earth. One had to do with the way liquids diffused without gravity. The other studied how accurately humans could throw objects in space. In the second experiment the astronauts put a Velcro target on a shuttle wall and then tossed a rolled-up sock, an orange, a bun, and a ball of tin foil at the target in order to see if the lack of gravity affected their aim. Marc Garneau participated in both studies, but the one that involved throwing the things was more fun. He also helped fix a Coca-Cola machine that failed to work as it should have in orbit. The machine was being carried on board as advertising for the drink company. Repairing it took a lot of time, but the astronauts finally got the thing to do what it was supposed to do.

MAPLE LEAF IN SPACE

* * *

Bob Thirsk also had an interesting and very busy trip into space. Like Marc Garneau, he had trained for years and he wanted to do a good job. He knew that hundreds of people would be watching him, including the grade five students at his old elementary school in Vancouver, British Columbia. The day of the launch, they were all seated on the gym floor, watching the blast off on a big screen at the front of the room. They were thrilled by what they saw and there was lots of cheering when the shuttle raced into the sky.

Bob had his family members with him in Florida that day, including his younger son, who was only five months old. Bob laughed later when he was told that even during the shattering roar when *Columbia* began to rise, the baby slept contentedly in his mother's arms.

A day or so before departure, Canada's newest astronaut wrote letters to his wife, his daughter, and his two sons. He reminded them that even though what he was about to do was very dangerous it was something he felt he had to do, and that he was still there with them in spirit. A friend gave the letters out after the shuttle entered orbit. Fortunately, all went well on the mission and in later years those letters became treasured souvenirs of an exciting time.

Bob Thirsk was born in British Columbia. Because his family moved often he lived in several towns and cities in that province. He graduated from the University of Calgary with a Bachelor of Science, and later went to McGill University in Montreal, where he became a medical doctor. In school he loved math and science, but he loved hockey just as much. He played the sport as a boy, and continues to do so as an adult. Today, he does some coaching, and still plays as often as he can. His hockey heroes are Bobby Orr, a former captain of the Boston Bruins, and Jean Beliveau, a long-time star of the Montreal Canadiens. In fact, Bob wore Orr's sweater on his first trip into space, and talked to Beliveau on a later trip.

Bob Thirsk also had heroes who were not sports figures. He was always fascinated by astronauts. In fact, when he was in elementary school he collected pictures of spacemen and women and pasted them on his bedroom wall. No wonder he decided that when he grew up he would like to go into space himself. His parents encouraged him to be whatever he wanted to be in life. For that reason, Bob feels that students should be able to pursue whatever career they

Canadian astronaut Bob Thirsk. This picture was taken at the Houston Space Center before Bob's historic mission to the International Space Station.

John Melady photo

want. Choosing to become an astronaut meant a lot of work, he says, but the results have been worth it. One of them is being able to fly through space, to look down at the beautiful Earth, and know that being an astronaut is a thrill and a privilege few people ever know.

The danger is real and all astronauts know that. In Bob's case, he told his family that he could die during the shuttle liftoff, during the flight itself, or during re-entry to Earth, when spaceships endure thousands of degrees of heat and are surrounded by fires that could kill in an instant. He discussed the dangers long before the mission began, and his wife and children accepted them. Even on the morning of his flight, as the countdown continued, he thought of the *Challenger* accident, and remembered some of his friends who were killed that day. He missed them, and was sad because of what happened, but was determined to do his job the best he could so that those brave men and women would never be forgotten.

Once Bob was in orbit, this mission was on the *Columbia*, the work began in earnest. In those 17 days whirling around the Earth, the men and women on board witnessed 16 sunsets and

FASCINATING FACT
The Hockey Shot in Space

One of the finest hockey players ever is the legendary Bobby Orr, the all-star defenceman who spent most of his career with the Boston Bruins. Bob Thirsk credits Orr with being an inspiration for him, not only in hockey but in life. The two have met, and Bob calls the Hockey Hall of Fame member a good role model, and "the best hockey player who ever played the game."

Orr is perhaps best remembered for a Stanley Cup final series goal he scored for Boston in the spring of 1970. There is a famous photograph of the goal that shows Orr flying through the air after having shot the cup-winning sudden-death goal. Bob decided to try to recreate the photo on his 1996 shuttle flight, so he contacted Orr and told him what he had in mind. Orr sent him not only a game jersey, but the Stanley Cup ring he had won in that Boston Bruins–St. Louis Blues series in 1970. Bob admits that he was in awe of Orr for years, but when he received the package containing the ring and sweater, was almost at a loss for words. When it was time, Bob put the sweater on, slipped the ring on his finger, and pretended to fly like Orr after scoring the spectacular goal.

16 sunrises *every day*, and they still performed admirably. Sometimes doing so meant rather unique challenges, particularly for the first-time fliers. Getting used to a weightless environment was one of them.

Bob says that during the first couple of days in orbit he really didn't feel as though he was floating. Instead, it felt as if he was freefalling, like a skydiver who jumps from a plane before his parachute opens. He remembers that the problem cleared up in a couple of days, but even while it persisted he still got his work done. He says that for the first while, he wanted to work with his feet toward the spaceship floor. Later on, he didn't care where his feet were.

During the mission, he and the crew did 43 scientific experiments in the Spacelab, including everything from testing the strength of a person's hand grip to examining hand-eye co-ordination to studying space sickness. These experiments were important because they would be used to help people cope with problems here on Earth. If you or someone you know gets carsick, you can be glad that the astronauts in space are doing all they can to find a method of preventing the problem.

When it came time to return to Earth, the six men and one woman on *Columbia* all wished their mission could have been longer. However, there would be other flights for most of them — including another for Bob Thirsk. Even though 13 years would pass before he went into space again, the wait would be worth it. His next journey would be truly spectacular.

From Iceland to Shuttle

When Bjarni Tryggvason was a little boy in Iceland, he didn't know what an airplane was — because he'd never seen one. That changed when his cousin came for a visit. The two boys enjoyed each other's company, played games together, and explored the area near the Tryggvason home. One day his cousin started talking about airplanes. Bjarni asked what they were. The cousin not only explained what he meant, he drew pictures of some planes for Bjarni and gave them to him to keep. Bjarni had those drawings for years.

But not so long after his cousin's visit, Bjarni not only saw a plane for the first time, but he flew in it — all the way from Reykjavik, the capital of his island home, to New York City. He and his family were moving to Canada, and the journey took them through the United States.

Today, Bjarni Tryggvason still remembers what his first flight was like. He had a window seat on the plane and spent almost the entire journey with his face pressed against the glass, looking at the sky, the clouds, and the Earth that was far below. The view thrilled him, but so did the plane. He thought it was wonderful; undoubtedly the most amazing machine he could ever have imagined.

But there was another thrill in store for Bjarni. Back in those days, when people got off a plane they walked down a stairway onto the tarmac and then crossed it to get into the airport terminal. On the ground at the New York airport Bjarni saw another kind of plane. This one was small, silver, and sleek, without propellers. Bjarni knew as he looked at it that it probably could fly fast. And he was right. The plane he saw was a jet plane, called a T-33, and it was being guarded. A couple of policemen stood nearby and no one was allowed to go near the futuristic-looking little aircraft — no matter how much they might have wanted to do so.

The Tryggvason family boarded another flight for Halifax, Nova Scotia. Soon, Bjarni and the rest of his family became Canadians. He lives here today, but has seen many other countries since he first arrived. In fact, he has seen the entire world — 190 times! The boy from Iceland who didn't know what a plane was grew up to become a pilot, then an astronaut, which allowed him to zip around the globe for almost 12 days on the spaceship *Discovery*. But before he travelled on a space shuttle got the chance to fly the same kind of fast jet plane he had seen that day in New York.

Canadian Space Agency photo

Bjarni Tryggvason, who flew on STS-85, was born in Iceland and still is the only astronaut from that country. He became a Canadian when he was a youngster.

Bjarni Tryggvason learned to fly in British Columbia, where the family moved after a couple of years on Canada's East Coast. When he was in high school, he belonged to an organization called the Air Force Reserve, and got to spend hours and hours around planes; cleaning them, maintaining them, gassing them up, and helping move them in and out of hangers. Sometimes friendly pilots gave him rides for free. It's no wonder he grew to love almost every plane he ever saw. But Bjarni didn't learn to fly until he graduated from high school.

One day, his mother asked him what he wanted to be in life. When he told her he thought he would like to be a pilot she told him that if that was the case, he should find someone who would teach him how to fly. That very day he took his mother's advice, drove to the nearest airport, and told a man he met there that he wanted to become a commercial pilot. The man he talked to told Bjarni that he could not become a commercial pilot right away. Eventually he could, but first he had to qualify as a private pilot, and in order to do that he had to take flying lessons.

Bjarni decided that was good advice and he began the training soon after. He still remembers what it was like to fly his first plane, sitting beside an instructor. He enjoyed that experience, but in less than a week got the chance to solo. He clearly recalls his first takeoff, his first circle out over the airport, and his first landing. They were all exciting, but he still found himself wondering what it would be like to fly a jet, like that little one he saw that day in New York.

In a way, Bjarni Tryggvason has always been in a hurry. He began his first flying lessons, finished them faster than his instructors expected, then wondered what to do next. In his spare time he learned how to fly float planes, the kind that land and take off on water. Later, after he qualified for his commercial licence, he piloted floats in various parts of British Columbia.

Even though Bjarni loved his work and was happiest when he was at the controls of an aircraft, he decided he needed an education in case there came a time when pilot jobs became scarce. He even thought of joining the air force so he could fly there, but in the end decided that he was too much of a free spirit to do all the marching, saluting, and taking orders that the military would have expected. For that reason, he went to university, graduated, then worked in several cities across this country. He was living and working in Ottawa when he first flew the jet of his dreams, the T-33. He also learned to fly a Harvard, an old Second World War training plane, at the Ottawa airport. Today he belongs to a club that flies Harvards that have been refurbished. They often fly in formation, where the wing tip of one almost touches the one beside it. The pilots also do loops and rolls for the crowds at air shows.

FASCINATING FACT
The T-33

The Lockheed T-33 Shooting Star, also called the "T-bird," is a two-seat version of the United States Air Force's first jet fighter, the F-80 Shooting Star. T-33s first entered service during the 1950s. Because of their two-seat design, which allows an experienced pilot to fly with a newer pilot, they quickly became the most popular jet trainer worldwide. In fact, they're still used today.

While he was in Ottawa, Bjarni Tryggvason heard about something that would be even more exciting than piloting a jet plane. He learned that Canada was about to have its own astronauts. Bjarni was interested immediately. From the time he was selected to be an astronaut, his life changed completely.

Even though Bjarni Tryggvason was among the first astronauts selected, it was several years before he got a chance to go up in a shuttle. There were many reasons for the delay, but a major setback was the terrible loss of the *Challenger* and its entire crew. When the time came for Bjarni to fly, he thought of those men and women who died, but didn't let that deter him. He told his wife, and their son, Michael, and daughter, Lauren, that what he was doing was dangerous but also important. They understood what he meant and supported him. However, once he had flown none of them wanted him to go to space again, and he chose not to.

Bjarni vividly remembers what it was like to sit on the launch pad, knowing that he would soon be in orbit, or he would be dead. At the time, he had spent over 4,000 hours as a pilot, and was impatient to get the shuttle into the air. He hoped the launch would be a good show for the spectators, and that it would be successful and safe. Fortunately, it was.

On the mission, STS-85, Bjarni Tryggvason did several scientific experiments. One of them had to do with the way fluids behave in space, compared to on Earth. The liquids could be almost anything, from water to orange juice to blood. On Earth, fluids flow in certain ways, like water in a stream, and scientists wanted to know if these same liquids would move the same way without gravity. The experiments done were lengthy and complex, and the results led to further study.

One of the problems with doing experiments in space is that shuttle vibration can affect the results. Bjarni helped design and perfect a kind of machine that eliminates those vibrations, called the Microgravity Vibration Isolation Mount (**MIM**). It's about a half metre by one metre in size. Eventually, the MIM would be used on the International Space Station.

During the mission, Bjarni participated in the usual activities expected from all crew members on board the shuttle flights. He took part in a question-and-answer session with students attending a summer space camp in Saskatoon. He told them that he was taller in space because of the lack of gravity, and that all astronauts experience the same thing when they go aloft. He mentioned that when his spine stretched in space, he experienced back ache, but that after a couple of days the problem disappeared. He also admitted having some nausea, or space sickness, but that he had been able to continue working in spite of it. The radio chat with the students took place as the shuttle soared 300 kilometres above the South Pacific Ocean. When the discussion ended, Bjarni looked out at the beautiful sea below and felt so privileged to be able to do what he was doing.

Even though he's no longer an astronaut, Bjarni Tryggvason is still busy. He is now a professor at the University of Western Ontario in London, but he continues to be interested in flying. He still flies Harvards for fun. He's also flown another kind of plane that is, in a way, the most interesting imaginable: the Silver Dart.

The Silver Dart is a reconstruction of the very first aircraft that flew in Canada. A man named John McCurdy was the pilot of the original when it soared above a frozen lake at Baddeck, Nova Scotia, on Tuesday afternoon, February 23, 1909. That first flight was a short one, but it was historic. One hundred years later, a group of individuals who were interested in flying and history made a new Silver Dart. The original had been destroyed long ago. The plane they made was not much more than wires, wood, and fabric, and the pilot sat outside on a bench, not in a warm cockpit.

But the flimsy-looking machine performed as hoped, and astronaut-pilot Bjarni Tryggvason loved the experience of getting it into the air. By piloting the Silver Dart he had flown on both the fastest machine ever, and the slowest. And neither of those was a T-33.

13 Operating on Rats

When new astronauts are chosen they are told that they must keep the information a secret from the media. The official announcement is made by the Canadian government in Ottawa, and the media must not know who has been hired until then. Every Canadian astronaut has gone through this procedure. The successful applicants are usually at home when they get the good news. Occasionally, that's not the case. It certainly was not for a man named Dave Williams. When he got the good news he was standing on a stage, in front of an audience of nurses, giving a speech.

On the day he became an astronaut, Dave Williams was working as a doctor at Sunnybrook Hospital, one of the best known and most important city hospitals in Canada. Sunnybrook is located in Toronto, where it handles serious emergency cases every day of the year. The men and women who work there are often called the best of the best, and Dr. Williams was one of them. In fact, at the time he was giving his speech he was director of Emergency Services at that hospital.

Partway through his talk that day, Dr. Williams's pager went off. He interrupted his address, excused himself, and stepped into a nearby hallway to answer the phone. The call had come from Ottawa. The person on the other end told Dave that he had just been selected as one of Canada's newest astronauts. More than 5,000 people had applied, but only Williams and two others would become part of the country's space program. The caller congratulated Williams, and just before the call ended reminded him that for the time being he should not talk publicly about the selection.

Dr. Williams hung up the phone, walked back to the microphone, and continued his talk. He later admitted that he was tremendously excited, happy, and thrilled to know that he would be an astronaut, but dared not let his feelings show. None of the nurses in the audience ever guessed how important that phone call had been to him. As soon as he could do so though, Dave told his wife Cathy Fraser the wonderful news. She was a pilot with Air Canada at the time and she fully supported him in his new career. Later on, after Dave and Cathy moved to Houston for his astronaut training, she continued to fly for Air Canada, and travelled back and forth to Toronto to do so.

Dave Williams was born in Saskatoon, Saskatchewan, but he grew up in Montreal. His father was a banker, his mother a nurse. Dave always felt that he acquired his love of medicine from his mother. From his father he inherited a spirit of adventure, and both have served him well. So did living and going to school in Montreal. That was where he learned to speak both French and English, our two national languages. All of our astronauts speak both.

Dave has always been adventurous, whether it was exploring, climbing mountains, hiking, canoeing, piloting a

Canadian astronaut Dave Williams is an avid photographer. He is pictured here taking photos of a shuttle in the days before the launch.

NASA photo

plane, or horseback riding. When he was a boy, he and his friends built rafts and sailed them, and he always loved to swim. He learned to scuba dive when he was 13, and was able to use that skill as an adult when he became involved in underwater exploration. In that role, he lived below the surface of the sea in a device called Aquarius, the world's only underwater research laboratory. But, before becoming an astronaut, being a doctor was always important and interesting.

As a medical doctor, Williams spent time in a number of places, and continued to upgrade his skills. He loved emergency medicine and did some of his finest work dealing with patients who came into hospital in critical condition. He was able to save the lives of individuals who probably would have died without his expert care, and reassure family members.

But even as he worked hard in busy hospitals, Dave occasionally wondered what it would be like to be an astronaut. Like so many others who have gone into space, he was influenced by the early American astronauts who, along with the Russians, were pioneers in perhaps the most exciting job of all. He saw those men and women on television, soaring in spaceships, passing through the outermost reaches of the Earth's atmosphere, and then going into orbit around it. He watched the moon landings and was fascinated as astronauts actually walked on the surface of the moon. He looked up at night, saw the mountains on the moon, and struggled to believe that any human beings could be there. But they were, and he wondered what it would be like to do what they were doing.

When Canada selected astronauts, Dave Williams decided to apply for one of those jobs himself. Later on, when he was chosen, his excitement — and his family's — was obvious. Of course, once the initial thrill passed, the real work of being an astronaut began. There were those weeks, months, and years of training, travel, pressure to perform, and often disappointment at not being named to a particular crew. Yet eventually Dave got his chance to fly, and joined six others on STS-90, on the shuttle *Columbia*. Being selected as one of the astronauts for his first flight will always be one of Dr. Williams' most exciting memories. All of the training, sacrifice, and work and worry were about to pay off at last. His shuttle left the Cape in the early afternoon of April 17, 1998. The Florida sky was clear and the launch was a good one.

As the spaceship soared into the heavens, Dave says that for him it was like the excitement of a child on Christmas morning. He knows he will never forget the experience. He also knows he will not forget how he felt — physically — as he flew into space. He recalls the changes the human body undergoes when there is virtually no gravity. As a doctor, he was fascinated by these changes, some of which included becoming taller in space, having his face become rather puffy, and how his inner ear was affected, resulting in changes to his balance. He also knew about and expected the onset of Space Adaptation Syndrome, or space sickness. He didn't get sick, but felt queasy at times.

As you've learned, without gravity body fluids, such as blood, shift in the body, particularly from the feet and legs toward the midsection, chest, and head. This causes the puffy face, and it often makes astronauts feel congested, as if they had colds. Sometimes it causes headaches as well as stomach upset. In most cases, the feelings of nausea disappear after a couple of days. There are now some medications that astronauts can take that lessen the problem. Dave had to do medical studies in a small laboratory on board so he took an anti-nausea medication — just in case. It helped.

The laboratory where Dr. Williams and others worked was called a Neurolab. It was located in the cargo bay of the shuttle. Neurolab was entered through a tunnel from the crew cockpit. Inside the lab there was room to do the experiments required of that mission. Dave participated in several studies, but one of his main jobs was to examine and perform surgery on some of the rats and mice that were on board.

FASCINATING FACT
Surgery in Space

The experiments that the astronauts do in space are important ways of gathering information that will help humans on Earth and in space. If people are going to live in space for long periods of time it's important to know how to treat the illnesses and injuries that will probably come up. Performing surgery in zero gravity isn't the same as doing it on Earth. Operating on small animals in zero gravity is helping scientists figure out techniques for operating on humans in space.

In the laboratory were lots of little critters, all of whom were playing a specific role in the advancement of medicine and science. Among them were the rats and mice — many of them pregnant — snails, fish, and hundreds of crickets. The humans on board also took part in several experiments.

In all, 26 life science experiments were done during the STS-90 mission. Every member of the crew was involved. Many of the animals, such as the rats and mice, did not complete the trip. They gave their lives for science. Some of their brains were removed so that the effect of weightlessness on them could be studied. The knowledge gained from them might be applied to human beings. No wonder Dr. Williams didn't want to be sick as he performed these delicate operations. By the end of the flight, most of the rodents were killed and their body parts preserved for later examination in universities.

In addition to experiments like the ones on the rats, several studies were done on crew members. In fact, 11 of the 26 experiments involved crew, although the doctors on board, including Dave, were usually the test subjects.

One of the experiments studied how the astronauts slept during the flight. Small sensors were attached to the bodies of the test subjects. Even though the sensors were somewhat uncomfortable, Dave and the others accepted them because they felt the study was important.

The effects of microgravity sometimes cause first-time astronauts to confuse a floor with a ceiling or a ceiling with a floor. Their balance in space may not be what it is on Earth. This loss of balance is similar to what older people experience sometimes when they fall for no noticeable reason. Astronauts study balance to figure out why people on Earth sometimes lose their balance for no known reason. This is one of the many things we hope to learn from space travel.

Dave Williams's first flight ended as it began — successfully. And while he was glad to be home safely, he found himself wishing that he might be able to return to space at least one more time. Years later, his wish came true in an amazing way! That story will be told in a later chapter.

14 A Canadian Woman Visits the Space Station

When Julie Payette was nine years old she decided she wanted to be an astronaut when she grew up. She and her classmates were sitting on the gym floor at her school in Montreal, watching a space launch on television. She remembers being thrilled by the spectacle and thinking the idea of going up in a rocket was exciting. But it was the astronauts that *really* interested her. They looked great in their spacesuits, heroic and oh so cool! Julie was so sure that she could be just like that, so she told her classmates she had decided to be an astronaut someday.

She began collecting photographs of astronauts, and newspaper and magazine articles about them. She put the pictures up in her room and imagined what it would be like to go up in a rocket. She loved talking about her plans, so much so that she now thinks some of her friends probably got tired of hearing her stories. But she never let her dreams die.

Her parents knew all about her wish and her determination, and they encouraged her. In fact, they were always very supportive. Most of her teachers were helpful as well, but they, like her parents, reminded her that she would have to work hard in school if she really wanted to fly someday. That was good advice.

Julie did her best in school and worked hard, even when she didn't like a particular subject. Often, when her classmates took breaks from their studies, Julie did not. Her marks were good, and she knew they had to remain that way because no one ever became an astronaut by failing in school. Even though there were obstacles ahead of her, she refused to become discouraged.

At the time, Canada didn't have astronauts, but to Julie that didn't seem important. Neither did the fact that she was a girl, and most of the American astronauts were men — men who spoke English. Julie only knew French at the time, but as she has often said, great obstacles are unimportant when you are nine. She continued to work hard in school, and played hard in every activity available.

Sports have always been important to Julie. She is an excellent runner. She often entered and won races against others in her own age bracket. She also played racquetball, swam, and participated in team sports. She particularly enjoyed swimming and was good at it, whether outside, in the summer, or in an indoor pool when the weather was cold. In the winter she skied, plunging down hills with a kind of wild recklessness. She was happiest when she skied fast, and the faster she went, the better she liked it.

But no matter how appealing the sport, no matter how good she became at it, she knew that the education she had would be the most important factor in reaching her goal. For that reason, she realized early on that science and math would probably be necessary for astronauts. Because of that, she even took extra courses in those subjects, which paid off later.

When she was only 16, Julie went away to school. She was awarded an international academic scholarship and studied overseas for two years. The school she attended is in Wales, and is called the United World College of the Atlantic. She was one of six Canadians admitted in her year. All of the students there were achievers and hard workers, and Julie thrived in that environment. The experience helped a great deal when she began taking courses at McGill University in Montreal. There, Julie earned a degree in mechanical engineering, and not long after enrolled at the University of Toronto where she earned a second degree in computer engineering. Both were important steps toward her long-held dream. She even went to Switzerland for a year to work, before coming back to take a job in her home city of Montreal. She was there when she learned that Canada was about to hire new astronauts. No one was surprised when she applied immediately.

The time between applying and being named was long, and Julie and the other applicants found the wait difficult. There were lots of rumours and speculation about who would be hired, but no one seemed to know for sure. After many weeks, the usual "short list" was made public, but there were so many names on it that the final choices did not seem much clearer. Then, at long last, the best applicants were picked, and Julie Payette was one of them. She had never been happier. She went to Houston and thrived on the training there. She is now Canada's second female astronaut.

The work leading up to flying on a shuttle is relentless, taxing, and purposeful. Julie flew for hours and hours on the reduced-gravity aircraft, the notorious vomit comet. She took deep-sea diving lessons, got her commercial pilot's licence, and learned to fly Tutor jets at the Canadian Air Force Base at Moose Jaw, Saskatchewan. These are the same kind of planes the Canadian "Snow Birds" use during their performances at air shows. Julie found them fast, exciting, and fun to fly. Finally, she was named to a shuttle crew.

Instead of being easier, the training schedule became more intense. There were so many important things about her flight that had to be looked after. Many of these seemed to be "last minute" items, but most of them could not have been done much earlier. Making sure that each crew member was absolutely certain what was expected of him or her was one important requirement. Other kinds of things, including food choices for the voyage, were made in the time shortly before departure. These could not be made months before. And in those last weeks before the mission, Julie got to know her other six crew members almost as well as she knew her closest friends. In fact, crew members do become friends and often good friends by the time the shuttle takes off. This is a positive development. After all, if serious problems crop up during any flight, it is generally better if you have friends looking after you.

On this mission, there were four men and three women. Julie was the only Canadian, and one of the men was Russian. The rest were Americans. Julie was a mission specialist at the time. That meant that she had a good understanding of operations on board the spaceship, and was prepared to assume whatever added responsibilities she might be given. Though the training had been intense, it had been fun at times, and interesting always. But by the time the mission was close to its start time, Julie and the rest of the crew were eager

Canadian astronaut Julie Payette is pictured during training. She is the veteran of two spaceflights and a role model for young women everywhere.

NASA photo

to get going. Training in Houston came to an end and the crew flew to Cape Canaveral for the final few days.

One evening, not long before the start of the mission, Julie did something she loved to do. She went flying, alone, up and over the Cape, and was able to see the beautiful shuttle *Discovery* that she would ride, standing gleaming and white in the light of the setting sun. The sight thrilled her and made her even more impatient to get going.

Finally, launch day came. Long before the scheduled hour, hundreds of spectators sought out the best places to watch the spectacle. The early morning air was unusually humid and uncomfortable, but that didn't deter the crowds. Area roadways were lined with cars, invited guests were wending their way toward Kennedy Space Center viewing positions, and local boaters used their knowledge of the area waterways to move as close as they could to the pad. In fact, one managed to sneak past Coast Guard patrols and got inside a well-publicized security zone. Luckily, he was spotted in time and ordered to get out of there. After every launch, the booster rockets from the shuttle fall into a particular area, just off the nearby Atlantic Ocean beach. This boater was right where the rockets would come down!

For each shuttle mission, families and friends of astronauts are grateful for the invitations they get to watch spaceships depart. Julie's parents and other family members, including her sister, were there. So were two nuns who had taught Julie in Montreal, and Aline Chrétien, the wife of then-Prime Minister Jean Chrétien. All were excited and keenly anticipating what they were about to see.

When the countdown concluded, the deafening roar of the rocket swept the crowd. Many covered their ears when the sound hit them, but no one looked away. In fact, it seemed as if everyone watched through the viewfinder of a camera or the lens of binoculars. The spectacle was magnificent and the noise drowned out the cheering from the joyful crowd. In no time, *Discovery* was in space.

The main purpose of the flight was to take supplies to the partially built International Space Station, which was unoccupied at the time. Before anyone could live there, food, water, and other essentials had to be put in place. *Discovery* was to be docked at the station to allow for the transfer of goods. The whole operation was a risky one, and the slightest mistake could be disastrous. The shuttle commander was aware of that. He had trained for months and months so that he could do his job with the precision required. Fortunately, he succeeded. Not long after, Julie Payette became the first Canadian to visit the space station. At the time of her visit, the station, which is now as long as two soccer fields placed end to end, was not yet completed. There was still work to be done before the first residents could move in.

Once the shuttle docked with the station, two spacewalks had to be done to attach cranes to the station's side. The cranes would be necessary when other spaceships arrived there in the future. Julie was in charge of directing the spacewalkers. She also operated the Canadarm. However, it was her visit to the ISS that she would remember most.

When the crew members of *Discovery* got inside the International Space Station, they found that it was both austere and noisy. The bothersome noise came from on-board fans. In order to quiet the racket, foam insulation was hauled through the connecting tunnel from the shuttle and permanently installed in the station. In all, about four tons of supplies were transferred from the shuttle to the station, including battery packs to replace ones that had been installed, but had stopped working. The astronauts also repaired a broken radio.

Soon, the three and a half days that *Discovery* crew members spent inside the station came to an end. The hatches between it and the shuttle were closed, and the visitors from Earth backed away and headed for home. For Julie Payette, the trip of a lifetime was almost over, but it only made her dream of another one someday. In the mean-

FASCINATING FACT
Visiting the Space Station for the First Time

Julie Payette was the first Canadian to visit the International Space Station. No one was living there at the time, but long-term residents arrived soon after. She remembers the place as being both cold and noisy. Because no one was living there yet, the station's two rooms lacked the warmth they would have once long-term residents arrived. Years later, Julie returned to the ISS and found that since being occupied it had changed a great deal.

time, she continued to work at the Johnson Space Center, and did whatever public relations duties her bosses at the Canadian Space Agency requested. She visited lots of schools, took part in television, radio, and newspaper interviews, and became the voice of Mission Control during other missions. In that role she was called the Capcom — or Capsule Communicator — the senior astronaut in Houston who talked to shuttle commanders as they sped around the globe. Though time went by, her dream of a second flight did not die. Eventually that dream would come true as well.

A Coke Machine and Other Things

Marc Garneau has been to space three times, more than any other Canadian. On the first flight he was a payload specialist, and was primarily involved in doing science experiments on board. That changed on his second flight, and would change even more on the final one. On both of his later flights he was a mission specialist. After his third trip, Marc retired from shuttle flying, but he had brought expertise to his job and honour to his country. For his role in space exploration, Marc Garneau will always be a Canadian hero.

Not long after his first flight, he began the rigorous mission specialist training in Houston. That meant hours and hours of classroom work, exhausting workouts in the gym, lots of shuttle simulator time, and painstaking practice sessions in the operation of the very sophisticated Canadarm. On his first trip into space, Marc was disappointed that even though the Canadarm was invented and built by Canadians, he was not qualified to operate it. But by the time he retired from space travel he had used it often. By that time, he was helping train other astronauts who were being introduced to the machine.

Marc also worked as a Capcom, the same role that Julie Payette performed. In fact, Marc was the first non-American who ever qualified for the job. It's an important specialty, because having an astronaut talk to the crew of the shuttles lends an air of authority and mutual trust to the operation. Because all shuttle commanders know the person they are talking to at Mission Control, they know they can rely on what he or she might say. This is particularly true if problems crop up on a flight. All Capcoms have a good understanding of things that can go wrong, and can give advice quickly, clearly, and in language that personnel on the shuttle are familiar with. Capcom training is not for everyone, of course, but those who are selected for the role must be highly professional. Some astronauts have never done the job, and in many cases have neither the aptitude nor the interest in doing so.

FASCINATING FACT
What Is a Capcom?

The full title is Capsule Communicator. The Capcom is generally the only person who talks to a shuttle crew while they're in space. The job is done by an astronaut at Mission Control, and the Capcom is often a backup for one of the people on the flight. If something goes wrong on a mission, NASA has always believed that the Capcom must have a good understanding of the in-flight situation. That's why an astronaut does the job. Marc Garneau was the first non-American Capcom.

Obviously, if Marc had not done a good job on his first flight he would never have had a chance to do the second or third. His professionalism was always obvious to the senior officials at the National Aeronautics and Space Administration (**NASA**) and at the Canadian Space Agency (**CSA**), who selected him for more than one mission. In the United States it's NASA that has the authority over everything to do with space, including assigning astronauts to flights. The organization has offices in many locations. The CSA is much smaller, and operates in fewer places. Ottawa is one of them, but probably the most impressive is the futuristic complex near Montreal. Anyone lucky enough to see this facility is always impressed. If you get the chance to visit, you should go. You will be glad you did.

Marc Garneau's first flight was on the shuttle *Challenger*, the same one that blew up over the Kennedy Space Center several months later. His other two flights were on *Endeavour*, and both were 10 days long.

There was a crew of six on Garneau's second mission, all men. Only one person was a rookie, while the commander on board had flown three times already. Marc felt much more confident in his own abilities than on his first flight. And because he was a mission specialist, and no longer a first-time flier, he had more responsibility over the operation of the entire shuttle, not just the various experiments that were being done on it.

In the months before the flight, Marc participated in a particular kind of training that was certainly much more risky than working in a simulator. In addition to being a pilot, he learned how to parachute and went on to do several free falls from planes. Most astronauts had not done much skydiving, but Marc believed that it was worthwhile. He felt that it made him concentrate, particularly if faced with an emergency on the jump. He knew he wanted to be ready in every possible way if the shuttle had serious trouble.

> **FASCINATING FACT**
> **The Shuttle *Endeavour***
>
> The shuttle *Endeavour* was commissioned in 1987 to replace the lost *Challenger*. The story of how *Endeavour* got its name is interesting. While the shuttle was under construction, elementary and high school students from all across the United States were invited to enter a contest to give the new spaceship a name. According to the entry rules, the new shuttle had to be named after a ship that had done important research in the past, or a ship that was famous in history.
>
> More than 200 years before Marc Garneau became an astronaut, an English explorer and sea captain named James Cook travelled widely on the Pacific Ocean, exploring unknown places and giving names to the new plants and animals he found on many of the South Sea Islands. Cook earned fame during his lifetime, as did the ship he sailed, the *Endeavour*. *Endeavour* was the most popular name entered in the contest and was declared the winner by then-President George Bush Sr. *Endeavour* first took off on May 7, 1992.

In the days before liftoff, Marc was in particularly good spirits, which reporters noticed. He admitted that his mood was good because he was really looking forward to the flight. And even though training continued right up to the moment of launch, most of it had been completed earlier. Finally, almost 12 years after his first spaceship journey, he was ready to go again.

The only thing that would be missing on this trip was that the shuttle would not be flying over Canada very much. Instead, it would circle the Earth of course at a more southern orbit. Marc told reporters that he expected to get brief glimpses of Canada, but that would be all. However, there were far too many things to do and see, and he knew he would enjoy the mission no matter what orbit was followed. He was even looking forward to all the work that lay ahead.

On the morning of the launch the weather was good, and the officials at NASA said that the liftoff was "clean," meaning that everything went according to plan. As the shuttle roared into the clear Florida skies the thousands of spectators cheered, and the white-hot fire from the great engines could be seen for long distances in every direction. By the time the crowd had finished staring at the heavens, *Endeavour* was already in orbit. Every member of the crew relaxed, knowing that the first really dangerous part of the flight was over. They unfastened their seat restraints and clambered out of their launch and entry suits. Already those who were closest to one of the 11 shuttle windows were thrilled by the sight of the beautiful Earth and the mountains, seas, deserts, and plains that lay far below. Some members of the crew cheered. Ear-to-ear grins spread across every face. They were in space at last! The years of work and worry had been worth it.

Among the spectators at the liftoff that day were students from Marc Garneau Collegiate in Toronto. They were all really excited by what they had watched, and they later told reporters that this flight was special to them because Marc had visited their school and they had met him. They all felt a

Marc Garneau waves to spectators as he prepares to board the Astrovan for his third and final space mission.

NASA photo

closer connection to this crew than any other that had flown. Because of what they had witnessed, several students said they might consider becoming astronauts when they got older.

In the cargo bay of the shuttle was a laboratory called a Spacehab. During the mission several experiments were done in it, most of them involving tiny creatures that had been brought along on the mission. There were starfish, things called blue mussels, and lots of baby sea urchins. Marc Garneau and other crew members would examine and work with these little beings in hope that such studies would someday help scientists understand and treat diseases suffered by humans. Because of the lack of gravity, particular experiments could be done that wouldn't be possible back on Earth. Many of the studies that Marc would be involved in had been designed by Canadian companies, and they would be anxiously awaiting the results. Even the aquarium that held many of the specimens was Canadian-designed.

There were also experiments inspired by students from across Canada. One of them was a study initiated at College Park School in Saskatoon. Students there wanted to know how such things as food colouring would diffuse in water when there was no gravity. Another study had to do with the development of items that would be useful for laser surgery here on Earth. There was an important one that related to Earthbound communications, and another of interest to the computer industry.

For Marc Garneau, the highlight of the mission was using the Canadarm to place what is called a Spartan satellite in orbit, and then to retrieve the device and move it back into the cargo bay. Marc did both of these things and later marvelled at how well the Canadarm worked. He had more success with it than with something else that was on board.

On the last day of November 2000, Marc left on his third spaceflight. The mission was STS-97. There were five astronauts on board, once again all male. Three spacewalks were made during the mission. The purpose of the voyage was to add more parts to the International Space Station. This mission would be the sixth construction flight to the structure, and Marc was thrilled to be going there. He had often wished he could visit the station before his days as an active astronaut ended. He was not only getting his wish, he was going to help build the thing.

FASCINATING FACT
Why Was There a Coke Machine in Space?

Because space flights are expensive, NASA welcomes projects from businesses that want what amounts to advertising, if they're willing to pay for it. On this mission, Coca-Cola had arranged to have one of their soft drink machines placed on board. Coke's rival — Pepsi — had said that Russian cosmonauts drank Pepsi while in orbit. Coca-Cola wanted to be able to brag that there was one of their machines on *Endeavour*, and that NASA astronauts used it when they wanted a Coke.

Unfortunately, the dispenser didn't work very well, and even after several crew members tried to fix it the results were still not great. Marc Garneau helped on the repair job, but he never felt that his future career would be as a soft drink machine repair person.

STS-97 began in the dark — shortly after 10 at night, Florida time — and even though it was late, thousands of people showed up to watch the launch. They were all thrilled by what they saw. This liftoff was one of the most dramatic imaginable, as the blinding flames below the shuttle, along with the monstrous clouds of white smoke and steam that surrounded the pad, all seemed magnified in the blackness. People who were up close were dazzled; those farther away said it was as if a great shooting star took off from Earth and then became the brightest one in the night sky. The throbbing roar of *Endeavour*'s engines echoed across the nearby beaches and far out over the waves of the Atlantic. The launch was absolutely spectacular!

On board the spaceship were two huge solar wings, or panels, neatly folded in the payload bay. They were expensive things, costing well over $90 million, but they would also be very important when attached to the space station. They would be unfolded there, where they would catch the rays of the sun and produce light and heat for the station. Without them, three rooms of the structure would remain cold.

In order for them to fit on board the shuttle, the solar panels had to be compact when closed. Once they were unfolded, they would be large, longer than a soccer field and wider than a classroom. Marc Garneau's job was to use the Canadarm to lift the wings out of the payload bay, and hold them in place while two crew members bolted them to the station. The men who were attaching the panels would be spacewalking. They also planned to put some other equipment in place.

The journey to the International Space Station went well — and the docking of the shuttle was just as successful. During the journey, the *Endeavour* astronauts were always in touch with Mission Control in Houston.

As always, every second of the voyage was being tracked at the Johnson Space Center. Through the Texas facility, *Endeavour* crew members were able to make live broadcasts from space. Marc Garneau talked to navy cadets, Girl Guides, and students from two Ontario schools who were following the mission at the Canada Science and Technology Museum in Ottawa. These young people had gathered there to watch and interview Marc, and were quite excited. Just talking to an astronaut in orbit is something very few people ever get to do. When they saw his face appear on the televisions screens in the room they cheered him loudly. Marc thanked them for their attention, answered questions, and talked about what it was like to be in space. He told them how lucky he was to have been given a chance to do something he had dreamed of doing, and that someday one or more of them might be doing the same thing. He also said that he was sure that in the not-too-distant future, human beings would be going back to the moon, and then on to Mars as well.

Soon it was time to return to work. On the day scheduled for the start of the solar panel assembly the spacewalkers made their preparations to go outside. In his role, Marc gently, carefully, and slowly lifted the wings from the bay and moved them to where they would be attached. He then directed the spacewalkers as they went about their work.

The wings were bolted onto the space station. When that was done Marc Garneau released the Canadarm. Once the massive blue and gold-coloured wings were carefully unfolded the necessary connections were made, and the vital electricity needed for the station began to flow. The entire hook-up operation had taken quite some time, but in the end was successful.

Shortly after the work on the wings concluded, the hatches between the shuttle and the International Space Station were opened, and crew members from *Endeavour* went into the station to visit the one American and three Russians who had been living there. They had been by themselves for 38 days, so their visitors were very welcome.

The men shook hands, laughed and joked, and enjoyed the get-together in the sky. But there was more work to be done, so they got at it right away. There were electrical hookups on the station that had to be fixed, computer problems to look into, and garbage from the station that had to be moved into the shuttle for transfer back to Earth. Finally, everything was complete. *Endeavour* headed for home, taking Marc Garneau for his last ride.

Blinded on a Spacewalk

Four months after Marc Garneau's final flight, his friend Chris Hadfield left for the International Space Station. He also flew on *Endeavour*, and he was also successful on an exciting journey. In fact, some space observers believe this mission was the most important ever flown by any Canadian. And while that may or may not be true, STS-100 — which launched on April 19, 2001 — did establish several historic milestones.

Blast-off time was in mid-afternoon. On board was an international crew: four astronauts from the United States, and one each from Canada, Italy, and Kazakhstan. All were men. Five were mission specialists, and Chris Hadfield was the lead member of that group. They flew for almost 12 days, orbiting the Earth 186 times, and travelled almost five million miles. They got a lot done on that trip.

The STS-100 mission was special for Canada. There was a Canadian on board and the flight had an important Canadian component. Carefully secured in the big payload bay of the shuttle was the 57-foot-long robotic invention called Canadarm2. This Canadarm would be installed on the space station. Chris Hadfield and an American mission specialist would do the physical work of putting the device in place. With upgrades and the necessary mainte-nance, it would operate from there for several years. The arm would soon become one of the most useful parts of the entire station. No wonder this mission was important to NASA, the Canadian Space Agency, and the thousands of men and women who built the arm. Installing it would be a highly complex and important step into the future.

The construction of the arm had been a long and complicated project, just as the preparation for its installation had involved thousands of hours of training for the astronauts who would be doing the work; a great deal of that training took place in the Neutral Buoyancy Laboratory at the Johnson Space Center.

As you learned in Chapter Five, practising in the pool is so important because it allows the astronauts to closely approximate conditions they will encounter in space. In other words, working underwater was much like being in space. Objects have to be moved slowly and carefully through the water and all activities have to be planned and choreographed to ensure success. To make the workplace even more realistic, an exact-sized replica of the space station has been placed in the pool. Every move an astronaut needed to make during station construction was practised in the water.

These sessions were long, grueling, and vitally important. For every hour an astronaut spends on a space walk they spend seven hours in the pool. In that time, every action done during the walk is practised over and over again underwater. It's exhausting, but absolutely necessary. To make the training as realistic as possible, in the pool astronauts wear spacesuits. The technical name for each of the suits they wear is Extravehicular Mobility Unit (**EMU**). Each one weighs about 127 kilograms (280 pounds) — no wonder wearing one while working in it underwater is so tiring. During these training sessions each astronaut has radio contact with Mission Control, just as they have on a spacewalk.

Finally the day of Chris's spacewalk came. After hours in the pool, liftoff from Cape Canaveral,

FASCINATING FACT
Extravehicular Mobility Units (EMU)

EMUs are basically spacesuits, comprised of 14 different layers of different kinds of fabric meant to protect the astronauts from the extreme conditions in space. The suits are mobile life-support units for the spacewalkers, providing them with oxygen, electrical power, heating and cooling to keep their temperature constant, and even a drink bag and waste elimination system. They also have a tether to keep the spacewalking astronaut from floating away into space.

and once the spaceship reached the International Space Station, work on the installation of Canadarm2 was about to begin and Chris Hadfield, the same nine-year-old kid who watched the first-ever moon landing on television, was about to become a spacewalker himself — the first Canadian who had ever done so.

In the hours before going outside the shuttle, Chris and his partner prepared themselves and their spacesuits for what is probably the most amazing thing any astronaut can ever do. Both men could hardly wait for the experience to begin. They wanted the walk to go well so they went over the checklist of moves again and again and again. Each man knew every second of spacewalking time had to be fully accounted for, and neither wanted anything to go wrong. They had complete confidence in each other and equal trust in the crew members who would remain inside, directing the operation, providing backup, and giving advice and encouragement. They also knew they would always be in direct and immediate contact with Mission Control in case anything went wrong.

Unfortunately, not long after he left the hatch of the spaceship, Chris Hadfield did have a problem — a serious problem. But first, he was thrilled to be out, and treasured every minute of the experience. He saw the beauty of the Earth below, the absolute blackness of the deep and velvet sky, the stars, the Southern Lights stretching to the Antarctic. He remembered floating out of *Endeavour*, and when he looked down, realizing that he was high above the Atlantic Ocean, floating across the eastern coastline of Brazil. A few minutes later, he found himself far from there, on the other side of the world.

And despite all the years of training and preparation for the spacewalk, Chris later admitted that he had not even imagined the wondrous beauty he would encounter as soon as he was outside the hatch. All the great openness of the Earth and sky was there before him. "I was not prepared for the overwhelming visual assault," he said later. "You have the entire universe in front of you. It is the most beautiful thing you have seen in your whole life. It is mind numbing to see, and then to try and tear yourself away from this raw, unprecedented beauty all around you and focus on the job you have been training for is physically difficult."

Chris felt he needed to soak up the view because what he saw was absolutely stunning. "It is a rare and tremendous human experience," he said. "I felt I had to take some time

Astronaut Chris Hadfield stands on the end of the Canadian-built Canadarm to work with the Canadarm2 during its installation on the International Space Station in April 2001.

NASA photo

and look at it and try to absorb as much as I could so I could make a slight *attempt* at trying to tell others about it."

But, because they knew their time outside was fleeting, Chris and his partner both had to force themselves to turn to the job that lay before them. They knew it would be difficult but worthwhile. Already, Canadarm2 had been lifted from the cargo bay. Slowly and carefully, Hadfield and his partner prepared to bolt this new space crane, as it is sometimes called, to the International Space Station. But as they worked, Chris realized that he had a problem — he was going blind.

The shock was something he will never forget. Here he was, 402 kilometres above the Earth, moving at 27,360 kilometres per hour, encased in a suit that in itself was a small spaceship, wearing heavy, multi-layered gloves, helmet, and visor, and unable to touch his face under any circumstances.

He explained what happened:

> I was working away, and suddenly my left eye became irritated. Then it started tearing up and stinging, like when you get raw shampoo in your eye. Your eye shuts and you have to rub it and flush it because you can't see out of it anymore. Well, my eye started doing that. Because I could not figure out what was causing the problem, I tried to work with one eye for a while, and I didn't tell anybody.
>
> The trouble is, tears need gravity, and drain because of gravity. That way, your eye clears itself. But without gravity, you just get a bigger and bigger ball of tear. Then it gets big enough so that it goes across the bridge of your nose and gets into the other eye. That's what happened to me. Soon both my eyes were blinded and I couldn't see out of either of them.

Chris was seriously worried, but he refused to panic. "I opened and closed my eyes, again and again, but they wouldn't clear, and the situation actually got worse. Now both were clouded."

While he tried to decide what to do next, Chris held onto the shuttle to steady himself, and talked to Mission Control, telling them he was going to have to take a break and explaining why. The technicians in Houston were worried that there might be some kind of chemical leak into Hadfield's helmet. In order to correct the situation, they told him to open a valve and let some oxygen out of his spacesuit. He did so, but nothing seemed to change. Fortunately, the problem got solved in another way.

Because his eyes were now stinging so much, larger and larger tears were forming in both of them. This continued for almost half an hour, but then something amazing happened. The tears started to evaporate, and the stinging became less and less. Another few minutes passed, and even though everything he saw looked murky at first, Chris realized that his vision was improving. The tears evaporated completely, and he was able to complete the spacewalk. Later, after tests had been done on his helmet and the residue of the tears from around his eyes, it was determined that the chemical he had cleaned his visor with had mixed with a bit of water from his drink container, causing the eye irritation. Since then a different kind of visor cleaner has been used.

On their first spacewalk Chris and his partner were outside the shuttle for over seven hours. During that time, they completed several tasks, from hooking up an antenna, to connecting cables to give Canadarm2 the necessary power it would need to bolting the machine to the space station. Once Canadarm2 was in place they began unfolding the arm. At the end of their work day, the two rather exhausted men returned to the shuttle and congratulated themselves. In spite of Chris's early problem they had completed all of the tasks assigned for the walk. They also laughed that even though they were in space, some things didn't operate any better than they might have on Earth — a power tool that was supposed to tighten the bolts that held Canadarm2 in place had not done what it was supposed to do. The two men had to tighten the bolts by hand, as if they were working in a garage on Earth.

During the time they were outside the shuttle, the spacewalkers were able to remain where they needed to be because they were held by foot restraints. Dramatic pictures were taken of them installing Canadarm2, and several of these photos ended up on televisions screens and in magazine and newspapers around the world.

Before the second spacewalk for the two men began, the hatches between the shuttle and the space station were opened, and the crews had their first visit together. After all the happy greetings, a cargo module that had been brought on the shuttle was emptied. The module was an Italian-made container called Raffaello, which carried food and other supplies for the station. In return, the garbage that had accumulated on the space station was put into the module for transport back to Earth. The unloading and reloading took some time because many things had to be transferred. In fact, Raffaello was still being packed with junk from the station when Chris Hadfield and his American partner began their second spacewalks.

Chris Hadfield's second spacewalk focused on hooking up permanent power connections between Canadarm2 and the space station, and doing several other checks of the electrical system.

For the journey from Earth to the space station, Canadarm2 rested in what was called a pallet, or a kind of cradle. Once the arm had been permanently bolted to the station,

FASCINATING FACT
Raffaello

Rafaello is also known as a Multi-Purpose Logistics Module (**MPLM**), which is just a fancy way of saying "moving van." There are actually three MPLMs: Raffaello, Leonardo, and Donatello (all named after Italian artists). They are used to transport supplies to the International Space Station. The MPLMs are cylindrical, about 6.5 metres long and 4.5 metres wide, and weigh almost 4.5 tons. Raffaello can carry up to 10 tons of cargo packed into 16 racks. The Italian Space Agency designed and produced the modules in exchange for Italian access to U.S. research time on the ISS.

the cradle, which was still attached to the arm, had to be removed and placed in the shuttle cargo bay for the trip back home. An astronaut on the space station operated Canadarm2, lifted the cradle, and passed it to Chris Hadfield, who took it with Canadarm and then gently lowered the pallet into the shuttle cargo bay. This "handing" of the pallet from Canadarm2 over to Canadarm was called a "Canadian Handshake" in space. Such a thing had never been done before. This activity, which took place high over British Columbia, was amazing, and Chris Hadfield was part of it.

Shortly after the handshake some important computer operations had to be done. Then there was a last visit to the space station before the hatches between the two spacecraft were closed. A day later, *Endeavour* headed for home. When the shuttle touched down at Edwards Air Force Base in California, everyone on board knew they had performed all their flight objectives. Their historic mission was over.

Wings of Gold

A few months before Steve MacLean was to make his second spaceflight, a terrible tragedy occurred. As you learned in Chapter Three, early in the morning of February 1, 2003, the shuttle *Columbia* was about to return to Earth after a long and successful journey. However, just as the spaceship began to descend it broke apart, and all seven crew members were dead before they knew what was wrong. At the time, *Columbia* was high above California, but because of its tremendous speed it was just over 20 minutes from landing in Florida.

A video that had been made by one of the astronauts just before the tragedy occurred was actually found beside a road in a rural Texas. Two searchers were checking the area and happened to notice a cassette in a ditch. On the tape were images of the astronauts working, smiling, and waving to the camera. Those pictures were a great comfort to the families of those who died. A wristwatch that a crew member intended to give as a gift to a friend at the end of the mission also turned up. Even though the watch crystal was missing, the hands were still attached, stopped at the exact minute the accident occurred.

Right after *Columbia* went down, then-United States President George W. Bush appointed a select team of investigators to look into what happened, and to suggest how such a disaster could be avoided in the future. The study continued for months, and for a time there were fears that no shuttles would ever fly again. However, after an official report was presented about the accident, its cause, and what the future should hold, it was decided that there would be more flights, as long as many new safety precautions were put in place. Once those improvements were completed, test flights were flown in order for officials to determine the new safety level. Finally, regular shuttle missions resumed, and Steve MacLean was told that he would finally fly — on *Atlantis*.

Despite the good news, there was still more disappointment and delay. For a time, no flights were made unless liftoff was in daylight. This was to allow every part of the shuttle's exterior to be photographed to make sure there were no unseen problems. Pictures taken during the day were believed to be more reliable than ones taken after dark. This made the scheduling of missions slower because there were only so many daylight hours.

Just when it seemed that Steve's flight was about to happen, mechanical problems were found at the launch pad. The matter was not really serious, but by the time it was corrected the flight had to be postponed until a later date. When the later date came another matter that *was* serious popped up.

The afternoon before the shuttle was good to go, a vicious electrical storm swept across central Florida and several thunderstorm cells were detected over the Kennedy Space Center. In fact, the biggest lightning strike since the shuttles began flying hit a lightning tower above the launch pad. It was later determined that *Atlantis* was not damaged, but the launch was delayed again so that technicians could check things out.

The people who prepare the shuttle for launch were still making all the necessary checks when yet another problem cropped up. A huge tropical storm called Ernesto had formed over the Atlantic. Since the launch pad at the Kennedy Space Center is only half a kilometre from the coast, there were fears that *Atlantis* could be damaged if winds from the storm reached hurricane force. The spaceship was hauled off the pad to be moved to safety inside the Vehicle Assembly Building. *Atlantis* never actually got back to the VAB. The big crawler-transporter that transports the spaceship only got partway there before the path of Ernesto changed so that the storm would bypass the Space Center. *Atlantis* was safe.

NASA photo

Prior to departing on the spaceship Atlantis, *Mission Specialist Steve MacLean adjusts his launch suit in the White Room at Launch Pad 39B. The mission he was about to fly was STS-115; it involved almost 12 days in space, his spacewalk, and orbiting the Earth 187 times.*

A day or so later, the shuttle was back on its launch pad being checked and rechecked to make certain it was still safe to fly. A few minor last-minute problems were corrected, the fuel tanks were filled, the crew was belted in, and finally *Atlantis* took flight. Steve MacLean was on his second mission at last — to the International Space Station.

Steve later admitted to being concerned about this flight. After all the delays, the threat of a hurricane, and the lightning strike, it seemed as if *Atlantis* might always be the centre of problems. Steve might not have been worried too much about his own safety, but he knew if anything bad happened during the mission it would be difficult for his wife and three children. However, in the hours before the launch, when everything checked out, he felt better.

Liftoff was at 11:15 in the morning, on September 9, 2006. The weather in Florida was favourable, and all went well. At the time, the International Space Station was 354 kilometres above the Earth, between Greenland and Iceland. *Atlantis* headed in that direction and reached orbit on schedule.

In the crew compartment of the shuttle, and back at Kennedy and in Houston, there was relief. And while everyone hoped all the problems were in the past, no one wanted to take any chances. *Atlantis* was checked out as much as any spaceship ever flown.

Soon after the shuttle was established in orbit, the cargo bay was opened, and a thorough inspection of the craft was begun. Crew members used the Canadarm and what was called a sensor boom at the end of it to examine the entire outer surface of *Atlantis*. Particular attention was given to the front, or leading edges of the wings, to the nose cap, and to the hundreds of tiles that make up the heat shield on the under surface of the spaceship. This shield is the main protector against the extreme heat of re-entry, when the shuttles return to Earth at the end of the mission. Fortunately, no problems were found, and the flight continued.

The main purpose of the mission, STS-115, was to transport a huge new part to the space station. This part, called a truss, weighs more than 17 tons on Earth and is as big as a bus. There were also batteries, another set of solar arrays, and some electrical items that were needed on the station. As always, the beauty of the Earth as seen from space, the lack of gravity, and the realization that they were aloft at last thrilled every crew member — but particularly those who had not been in space already. And even though *he* had been here before, Steve MacLean found the whole thing as marvelous as it was the first time. Unlike his last trip, this time he would be doing a spacewalk. That alone pleased him as nothing else could.

Atlantis docked at the International Space Station on day three of the flight. The six astronauts who had just arrived were warmly welcomed by the three inhabitants of the station. The crews had a brief reunion, but soon they were ready to get down to work. The first task was to move the much-needed shuttle cargo to the station. That done, the all-important transfer of the huge truss began. Two astronauts on *Atlantis* used the Canadarm to lift the truss from the payload bay.

FASCINATING FACT
Powering the ISS

There are no power plants in space, so the ISS uses the sun to generate its electricity. Since the space station is in space, where there are no rainy days, that might seem easy to do, but it's not as simple as you might think. The ISS orbits the Earth once every 92 minutes. For up to 36 minutes of each orbit the Earth is between the Station and the sun, blocking out the light. That means that the ISS spends almost 40% of its time in the shade. To provide the Station with continuous power, a system of batteries had to be developed to store up extra energy during the sunny times that can be used during the shady periods. The huge solar "wings" that Steve MacLean helped install collect solar energy as the ISS moves around the sunny side of the Earth. Once the Station moves into the shade, the batteries take over, keeping the power continuous. The Station's solar system can generate up to 128 kilowatts of power, enough to supply 64 homes on Earth.

Then Steve and a crewman from the station used Canadarm2 to grapple the truss and position it for its ultimate position as part of the station itself. This made Steve the first Canadian to operate Canadarm2 in space — a memorable accomplishment that was widely reported in newspapers and on television and radio programs on Earth.

The following day was what NASA called "Installation Day" at the International Space Station. Two American members of the *Atlantis* crew spent several hours spacewalking to begin the process of attaching the truss. Large bolts were needed to hold it in place, and Steve MacLean used Canadarm2 to position the truss so that the spacewalkers could make the necessary connection. The operation was done quickly and without problems.

The following day, Steve did his spacewalk. "It was the most amazing thing," he said later. "The two dimensional window of the shuttle is nothing compared to the peripheral vision you have within your helmet outside."

Steve was at a loss for words when describing the experience of a spacewalk — and no wonder. Very few human beings in the entire history of the world have been fortunate enough to participate in such a thing. Steve recalled,

Your perceptions of speed, of height, and so on are far more accurate outside than they are inside. There is a world of difference between the two. But I won't say it's overwhelming, because if it had been overwhelming to me, I would have made a mistake in the first 10 minutes. But I really focused so that I would not make a mistake at any time — but especially in those first few minutes. Being out there is amazing.

During their spacewalk, Steve and his partner spent most of the time adjusting a large mechanical joint that would allow the solar arrays at the station to point toward the sun to collect solar power for the station. The joint the men worked on is as big as a car, and some of the bolts they had to fasten just would not turn. There were several television pictures of Steve working on one bolt in particular. His helmet camera focused on what he was doing, and even with the big, bulky white spacesuit he was wearing, anyone watching him on TV could detect his sense of frustration with the job. Eventually, he was able to get the bolt to work.

Two days later, a third and final spacewalk was done to spread the giant solar arrays' wings. Some said they looked like "wings of gold." Several crew members, including Steve MacLean, did interviews with news organizations on Earth. Finally, the last of the supplies were delivered to the space station, including 40 kilograms (90 pounds) of oxygen. In turn, unneeded equipment and trash from the station was packaged and loaded for its return to Earth. Crew goodbyes were said, the hatches between *Atlantis* and the station were closed, and the shuttle moved away from the largest-ever Earth-made object in the sky. In all, there had been six days, two hours, and two minutes of joint operations between the two spaceships.

The shuttle was checked over before beginning its trip back to Earth. The re-entry was safe, and early in the morning on Thursday, September 21, *Atlantis* landed on Runway 33 at the Kennedy Space Center. All crew members were happy to be home. They were also happy and surprised when, four days later, all of them, along with their families, were invited to the White House in Washington. That was because the President Bush wanted to personally thank them for the successful completion of a magnificent mission.

18 Fire Alarm in the Sky

Before Dave Williams went into space for the first time, he trained to do a spacewalk in case of an emergency. Fortunately, the other astronauts who did walks on the mission did so safely. If anything had gone wrong, Dr. Williams would have been called upon to assist. Because that didn't happen, he was never outside the shuttle. That changed on his second mission, when he did three spacewalks, the most any Canadian has ever done. They were all construction jobs on the International Space Station.

Dave's flight launched from Cape Canaveral on an extremely hot evening. There were a few light clouds over Florida that day, but they had pretty much disappeared by launch time. The humidity was excessive, and spectators sought any shade they could find. There was no breeze either, so the heat lay like a damp blanket over the thousands who were there. None of them seemed to mind because this launch, like all launches, promised to be an exciting one.

The spaceship *Endeavour*, one of the three remaining shuttles in NASA's fleet, was ready to go. The fuelling was done, the astronauts were on board, and the technicians doing the final check before departure were swarming over the machinery on Pad 39A. All the photographers were prepared to take pictures of the spaceship as it blasted from Earth. The television cameras focused on the stack: the shuttle, the solid rocket boosters, and the external fuel tank.

An American flag near the big digital clock that indicates the progress of the countdown hung limp from the pole that held it. The only partial snag involved the shuttle crew hatch. It didn't seem to close properly at first, but after workers in white suits made adjustments to the locks it was secured. In those last seconds just before liftoff, the mechanical arms of the support structure pulled back from *Endeavour*, the countdown moved to zero, and the great engines of the spacecraft roared into life. In seconds, the entire launch pad disappeared from view as billows of steam, roaring flames, smoke, and towering exhaust clouds swirled up and outwards. In the middle of all this, the shuttle seemed to wobble at first, but then as millions of litres of fuel began to burn with a shattering roar, the massive machine began its journey to the skies. All across the viewing areas waves of cheers, excited laughter, applause, and even tears of joy were common.

For a long time the spectators watched the spaceship go, taking more pictures, cheering, and forgetting the heat of the day for a few minutes. Soon everyone headed home, creating a traffic jam. Far above, the seven astronauts were happy to be underway. Dave Williams was as thrilled as the rest of the crew. He had waited a long time for this day — but so had a lot of other people.

On the day the spaceship *Challenger* exploded, one of those who died was a young woman named Christa McAuliffe. She was a teacher who was going to be teaching classes from space. As we know, she never got the chance to do so, but the dream never died, especially for Barbara Morgan, who was Christa's backup on that sad day. Barbara continued to work for NASA and eventually became a fully qualified astronaut. To help make Christa's dream come true, Barbara flew. Like Dave Williams, she was delighted to be on the mission. She was going to teach lessons on the shuttle to be broadcast across the United States and elsewhere to thousands of young people.

FASCINATING FACT
Christa McAuliffe

Christa was born September 2, 1948, in Boston, Massachusetts, and grew up in nearby Framingham. Christa was a junior-high-school teacher, who taught history, civics, and social science. After beating out 11,500 other applicants, she was selected to take part in NASA's "Teacher in Space" program in 1985. She was scheduled to teach two lessons from space on the 1986 *Challenger* mission. She was survived by her husband, Steve, and their two children, Scott and Caroline. She and the rest of the astronauts who perished on the *Challenger* were posthumously awarded the Congressional Space Medal of Honor.

NASA photo

This picture of the shuttle Endeavour *docked at the International Space Station was taken by a crew member during the third spacewalk on STS-118. Both Canadarm and Canadarm2 can be seen in the photograph — with the Earth and space as backdrop.*

MAPLE LEAF IN SPACE

As you learned in Chapter Thirteen, on his previous flight Dave had participated in several medical experiments, and even performed operations in space. On his second mission, STS-118, his main job would be to help build the space station. Most of the work had already been done, but the completion of the biggest structure ever built in space took a long time. It was also risky, and required detailed co-ordination and years of preparation. By the time *Endeavour* had docked at the station, Dave was ready to go. So were the other astronauts who would be working with him.

For Dave Williams, spacewalking was a wonderful experience. To explain what it was like, he said it was like riding on a motorcycle compared to riding in a car. Being in a spaceship was like being in a car, in an enclosed space where you just see what's outside. Spacewalking is like being on a motorcycle, where you're actually outside. When he was doing a spacewalk, Dave felt that he could see and appreciate the beauty of the Earth and the blackness of space in a more dramatic way than was possible inside the shuttle.

While Dave was circling the Earth, far below him, his wife, Cathy, his son, Evan, 12, and his daughter, Olivia, nine, were all thinking of him and were thrilled for him. They lived near the Johnson Space Center, and while Evan and Olivia knew the astronauts who were their neighbours, the fact that their *own father* was on this mission was really special. They hoped for success in what he was doing, of course, but knew that they would be happiest when he got back to Earth — safe and sound.

In the middle of Dave's first spacewalk something happened that would terrify most people. The fire alarm on the space station rang! Dave remembers being startled by the noise, and briefly wondering how to react. Fortunately, there was no fire, and within seconds the astronaut directing the walk told Dave and his partner that there had been a false alarm. Nevertheless, while the matter was unexpected and unwelcome, both astronauts continued with their work. At the time, they were perched far out on the side of the station, concentrating on the job. Even though the alarm incident passed quickly, both remembered it.

Dave also remembers how well coordinated he and his partner were with the crew member who was inside directing them, Tracy Caldwell, a young American woman who is an absolute professional in her job. Both men on the spacewalk had to learn not only how to work with each other, but also how to take the directions that Tracy gave them. Dave has since said that the spacewalk was an unqualified success, due in large part to how well Tracy handled it.

Dave also remembers that not long after the alarm went off he and his partner were back at the job, concentrating completely on what they were doing. They were interrupted again, but by something different entirely and truly wondrous. They were 563 kilometres above the Earth, directly over the Gulf of Mexico, when Tracy suggested they look down. Both did and found themselves staring directly into the eye of a giant hurricane. As he looked at the awesome fury of nature, Dave Williams said that he knew that both he and his partner would have

Canadian Doctor Dave Williams waves to reporters as he walks with Barbara Morgan to the Astrovan. Barbara Morgan was the backup to Christa McAuliffe, who lost her life when the Challenger *exploded above the heads of thousands of horrified spectators at Cape Canaveral.*

John Melady photo

missed the spectacle entirely had Tracy not drawn their attention to it, because, as he later said, "Spacewalking is not only a huge physical challenge, it is a big mental challenge as well. In order to remember the sequence, the choreography and so on, you can't afford to let your attention wander."

Dave Williams was a model of concentration on the entire mission. He and other space-walkers were responsible for many things during its course. Among them was the replacement of one of the station's four big gyroscopes. These machines weigh about 272 kilograms (600 pounds) on Earth, but in space could be easily manoeuvred by a single person. The gyroscopes help control the position of the station in space.

In addition to this work on the station and outside it, crew members of *Endeavour* participated in media and other interviews from space. Sometimes these were with news organizations, sometimes with schoolchildren, and at other times with politicians in astronauts' hometowns and elsewhere. Because she was the first teacher in space, Barbara Morgan had to juggle far more interview requests than she had time to handle, so Dave Williams helped her out and took part in many interviews with her. Some of them were for radio, while others were televised. One was for a place in the state of Idaho, where Barbara had taught. And even though Dave was never a teacher there, he was asked to participate because of his easy broadcast manner and his ability to talk to, and understand, young people. The kids asked questions about what it was like to be weightless, how the crew got fresh air on the shuttle, what planets and stars looked like when viewed from space, why people became taller in space, and more.

Another broadcast involved Canadian schoolchildren in Saskatchewan. During that 20-minute session, Dr. Williams answered the questions put to him, and then talked to his audience about their role in the future, how they should learn to recognize the explorer within themselves, and how each might play an active role in whatever their generation does in space.

Toward the end of the mission, and not long before the shuttle was about to leave for home, an unexpected problem arose. The hurricane that Dave and his partner had seen earlier looked as if it might prevent a safe return to Earth. In fact, the storm, which had been given the name Dean, was moving across the Gulf of Mexico and looked like it headed for the Texas coast and inland toward the Johnson Space Center. If that happened, Mission Control could have been affected, or even closed for a time. As a precaution, some emergency people from Houston prepared to fly to Florida so they could monitor the flight from there if need be. As an added safety precaution, NASA managers elected to shorten the STS-118 mission by one day. Their priority was to get *Endeavour* down safe and soon.

In the end, Hurricane Dean was not a problem, and Dave Williams' second and final mission ended without incident. A few months later, the emergency room doctor who became one of Canada's most famous astronauts declined any future shuttle missions. He went back to his first love — the healing of human beings. He is still doing just that.

19 A Dangerous Repair Job

Some of the most spectacular photographs ever were taken by an amazing invention called the Hubble Telescope. Named after American astronomer Edwin Hubble, this instrument was placed in orbit in 1990 by crew members on the spaceship *Discovery*. All the scientists who built the telescope were sure it would provide the best-ever views of the heavens. But they were shocked when the pictures that came back were out of focus, fuzzy, and disappointing. There was a technical problem with the design.

The manufacturers were sure that if the flaw could somehow be corrected the pictures made would be clearer and more useful than those taken from any telescope on Earth. Here, even telescopes placed on mountaintops have to contend with lights, weather conditions, and the atmosphere itself, all of which interfere with the picture clarity. Because Hubble was not on the Earth there shouldn't have been interference. The atmosphere was not the problem — the telescope was.

There was lots of discussion about what to do about the telescope, and there were two lines of thinking. The first was to abandon the telescope. The second was to send a shuttle and see if the astronauts could make repairs. Until a decision was made, NASA was severely criticized because this very expensive machine seemed to have been a waste of money. The dispute continued for many months until finally it was determined that they should at least try to fix Hubble. NASA knew that such an operation would be costly and dangerous, but despite that the work should proceed. Finally, after three years of debate, the shuttle *Endeavour* and a seven-member crew was launched. They caught up to the Hubble and examined it. They found several problems, but the biggest one was a defect in the most important mirror. Fortunately, the astronauts on the mission, with guidance from astronomers on Earth, were able to do the necessary repairs.

For the next few years, Hubble sent back photographs of the heavens that were both detailed and stunning. They allowed scientists to learn more about the universe and our planet's position in it. The pictures continued to be returned for some time, even as other missions went back to Hubble to make more improvements. But finally NASA officials determined that further repair attempts were just too dangerous. Many people felt that the machine had come to the end of its productive existence; but not everyone.

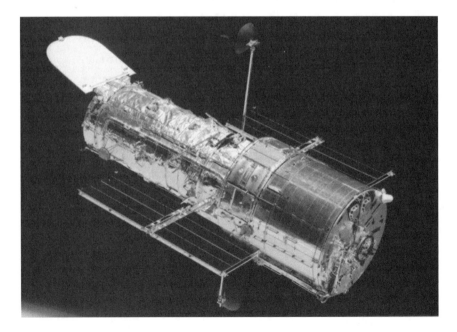

There were many scientists and astronomers who were sure that with new technologies, and by using the most advanced computers in the world, the Hubble could be rebuilt, extending its usefulness for several more years. However, no one wanted to have astronauts risk their lives

The Hubble Space Telescope as photographed by a crew member on the shuttle Atlantis *during the dangerous repair mission.*

NASA photo

for something that might not be worth it. Two shuttles had already been blown out of the sky, and 14 brave men and women lost on them. Particularly after the *Columbia* disaster, the idea of going back to Hubble was looked upon as foolishness. Other telescopes could be used without endangering lives.

Still, there were astronomers and high officials, at both NASA and the European Space Agency, who had helped build the Hubble and were sure a repair and upgrade mission could be undertaken with minimal risk to the crew — though the danger could never be completely eliminated. Several possibilities were considered and finally a solution was decided upon.

Two space shuttles would be prepared for flight. Both were taken to the launch pads at the Kennedy Space Center, however, if all went well on the Hubble mission only one shuttle would blast off. The other would stay on the ground in case it needed to be used as a rescue vehicle. If anything went wrong on the trip to Hubble, or during the

> ## FASCINATING FACT
> ### The Hubble Telescope
>
> Hubble was launched in 1990. The telescope circles the Earth at a speed of 8 kilometres per second, and each orbit takes 97 minutes. The telescope works by focusing light through its two mirrors, the main mirror in the back (the one that had to be repaired) collects the light first and reflects it onto the secondary mirror, which is positioned to send light to the focal point, where the pictures are taken.

repairs, the rescue shuttle would go and bring the first crew home. Even though the International Space Station was in orbit it was too far away from Hubble to be used as a safety port.

The rescue scheme had never been tried before, and no one really knew if it would work at all. It would be terribly risky, which every astronaut on the repair mission knew. Nevertheless, the repair flight, on the shuttle *Atlantis*, was a go.

One of the mission specialists on board it would be a young man named Drew Feustel, whose presence was of special interest to Canadians. Drew was born in the American state of Pennsylvania, but grew up and went to elementary and secondary school near Detroit, Michigan. After he graduated from high school he went to university in the United States. In his final year he met the young woman who would become his wife. She was a Canadian, and she and Drew moved to Canada, where he studied at Queen's University in Kingston, Ontario.

After Queen's, Drew stayed in Canada to work. One evening, when he was at home watching television, he saw a program about the way Canadian astronauts were chosen. Several people, such as Dave Williams, Julie Payette, and Chris Hadfield, were mentioned. Drew was interested in what he saw — so interested that he phoned Chris Hadfield, who invited him to come to Houston to look around. Chris even became his guide there. Because of that trip Drew became an astronaut. He later became a Canadian. Eventually, he was named to the crew of STS-125, the shuttle repair mission to the Hubble Telescope. By that time, he and his wife, Indira, had two sons, Ari and Aden, both of whom were born in Canada.

Drew knew that his wife was aware of the danger involved in this trip into space, but he wanted to be sure his sons knew as well. He talked to them about the risk involved, and explained that if something went wrong he might not be coming home again. But he also told them how much he believed in what he was doing. He said he hoped that in their lives they would find something just as important that they were committed to, and that would mean as much to them. Both boys knew they wouldn't relax until their father was back on Earth again, but understood his point of view. Their pride in him increased.

The departure of *Atlantis* came in the early afternoon on Monday, May 11, 2009. The skies were clear for the launch in Florida. There were seven on board the shuttle, six men and one woman. All of them looked forward to the task ahead, and were confident that it could be done. They also knew that astronomers around the world would be following their progress. No one on board wanted to let anyone down.

As the spaceship soared into the spring sky, the telescope they hoped to repair was directly overhead. In less than nine minutes, *Atlantis* was in orbit and streaking toward it. STS-125 would last almost 13 days. The rendezvous with the telescope would come two days into the flight.

As is the case with every journey into space, the first hours aloft were spent checking the shuttle and its cargo to ensure that all was well. Both the ship and its precious payload had survived the launch without obvious problems. Shortly after noon on Wednesday, May 13, *Atlantis* Mission Specialist Megan McArthur used the Canadarm to hook onto Hubble and get it in place for repairs. The initial step on the dangerous journey had been a successful one.

On this mission Drew Feustel would be making three spacewalks, and he was pleased and honoured to have been chosen to do them. Along with the rest of the crew, he had trained for months and months for the tasks ahead and did not want to disappoint. He took the job seriously — even more so perhaps than he did anything he had ever done.

The planning timeline for each repair step seemed to constantly change, but after much trial and error back on Earth, the exact order in which things would be done was decided. Drew and his partner, John Grunsfeld, would do the first spacewalk. They would install a new device called a Science Instrument Command and Data Handling System, which the spacewalkers generally just called a box. They compared the work to the changing batteries — the old "box" would simply be removed from Hubble and the new one would replace it. After that had been done, Hubble would perform better and would be able see farther into space. For Drew the thrilling part was being outside, and riding the Canadarm.

In the days that followed more parts were changed on the telescope — gyroscopes and other instruments to help Hubble point itself into distant space so that new stars and other faraway objects could be detected. The work on the mission was made more thrilling because each crew member on *Atlantis* understood and appreciated the benefits to the world that their efforts made possible. And even

Doctor Drew Feustel was a mission specialist for the dangerous mission to refurbish the Hubble Telescope.

John Melady photo

when one or more of the astronauts were not directly involved with upgrading Hubble, they were all contributing to the mission and to a safe flight. For example, Megan McArthur and another crew member spent considerable time doing detailed inspections of the heat tiles under the spaceship. As you now know, every one of them is vital in the fiery race through the atmosphere on the trip back to Earth.

Drew Feustel and John Grunsfeld installed additional replacement parts on Hubble during their second spacewalk. One of these was a kind of "contact lens" for the big telescope. The part is about the size of a telephone booth, and it weighs 386 kilograms (851 pounds) on Earth. In space, of course, the "lens" is considerably lighter. While they were outside the shuttle the two men also repaired one of the telescope's main cameras, which had not worked in a couple of years.

Finally, exactly one week after *Atlantis* was launched, Drew and John became the last human beings who would ever touch the famous telescope they had come to repair. On their third spacewalk, which lasted seven hours and two minutes, they did several things to Hubble to make it ready to perform the way its manufacturers intended. We don't know for sure, but maybe they patted the telescope one last time and said a final goodbye to it. The great Hubble Telescope was fixed again, and should be sending magnificent pictures back to Earth for many years to come.

The dangerous repair mission concluded safely — and the rescue shuttle did not have to be used, perhaps the best news of all. Also good news is that Drew Feustel has been named as a crew member for STS-134. That mission will take him to the International Space Station, where he will have the chance to walk in space again! If all goes well, that should happen in the spring of 2011.

20 Canadians Meet in Space

The first time that Julie Payette returned from space, she told anyone who asked that she hoped to go on a second flight sometime in the future. That second flight happened in the summer of 2009, when she flew on the shuttle *Endeavour* for STS-127. She had trained for a long time for the mission, and was fully prepared for whatever lay ahead. By then, more than training alone was expected of her. She had become an especially important representative of the Canadian astronaut group.

When Roberta Bondar retired, Julie was left as the only Canadian woman with flight experience. Because of that, she was called upon to do more public relations work than she otherwise might have. She gave speeches, worked on NASA projects, helped train new astronauts, dealt with the almost endless media demands, appeared on television programs across Canada and elsewhere, and travelled far and wide. In fact, so many people wanted to see her, meet her, take her picture, and even touch her, that people at the Canadian Space Agency at Montreal had to limit the requests. They knew that Julie always worked really hard at her job, but they also knew that she could only do so much. She was a young mother and had to be allowed *some* private time with her husband and their two sons. As it was, many people wondered how she ever managed to do all the things asked of her.

But she was certainly well trained and ready when the time came to return to space. Her second mission was sometimes called a construction trip, because during their time in orbit the astronauts would be adding parts to the ever-bigger International Space Station. The ISS was no longer the same station that Julie had visited 10 years earlier, before it was occupied. Since then, it had become much larger, and humans actually lived there; one of whom was Bob Thirsk. He would arrive shortly before she did, flying on a Soyuz, the spaceship used by the Russians. Julie looked forward to seeing Bob, and learning how he liked both his flight and the idea of living in space for a long time.

On her second mission, Julie was the flight engineer on board the shuttle. To do her job, she worked on the flight deck, seated between the commander and the pilot. She looked upon this as a great opportunity; perhaps the best any mission specialist could want. She got a chance to help manoeuvre the shuttle in flight, and assisted in docking and undocking from the space station. She was in the same seat for both the liftoff at the Cape, and for the return to Earth at the end of the 16-day trip. She read important checklists and crosschecked them, which is done in commercial planes too. If there were any problems, one of her jobs would be to do her best to help solve them. She was regarded as a very important member of the flight team in everything she did.

STS-127 was also quite historic from a Canadian perspective. Julie knew that and did her best not to let her country down. Foremost among the many "firsts" on the mission was the chance for two Canadians to meet in space. Julie knew Bob Thirsk well and looked forward to seeing him in such a unique situation. There were also a number of unique things about her mission.

Julie would be the first Canadian to use robotic systems from three countries. She would not only operate both Canadarm on the shuttle

FASCINATING FACT
A Woman We Admire

Julie Payette is now our only Canadian female astronaut. She has flown twice, and is deeply admired by people across the country. She is, and has been, a delightful role model for many. When time permits, she talks at schools across the country. Every time she does this, students pay close attention. She is always applauded loudly and after every speech she finds herself surrounded by young people who ask questions, seek her advice, take her picture, and ask for her autograph.

and Canadarm2 on the station, she would also use a third, smaller arm that had been jointly made by the United States and Japan. She would assist in the delivery of scientific equipment to the station, some of which would be used to help researchers on Earth understand the way liquids diffused, or spread apart, which could benefit the Canadian oil industry. There was also equipment being delivered that would help in experiments dealing with blood pressure in humans, and why we sometimes faint when our blood pressure is not what it should be.

During the docking, Julie and Bob would also be part of the largest group of astronauts ever together at the space station at the same time. There would be 13 people in all: seven Americans, two Canadians, two Russians, one person representing the European Space Agency, and one individual from Japan. Not since space exploration began had such a thing happened.

The beginning of the mission was delayed a number of times because of technical problems and bad weather in Florida, but when the shuttle finally did take off the launch was flawless. On board, the flight crew members were pleased to get airborne at last. They were in space in no time, and once there, quickly set about working through all the steps they had practised so often. But it was after docking at the International Space Station that the real work began. In all, five spacewalks had to be done in order to install the equipment delivered in the cargo bay of the shuttle. Julie Payette was involved in the transfer of every item.

One of the things that had to be moved from the shuttle and then bolted to the station was a JEM Exposed Facility, which is a kind of platform where experiments would be placed outside of the station to be exposed to space. The astronauts use a kind of short form when they talked about this apparatus — they called it "Jeff." The other things that had to be removed from *Endeavour* also had complicated names. One was a Vertical Cargo Carrier, so crew members nicknamed it "Vic." Another was the Japanese Logistic Element, which became "Jelly." All of these short forms made it easier when things had to be moved and installed.

Each of the installations was made; every one of them requiring close attention. Movements had to be slow and careful. Of course, all this was happening as the station, the shuttle, and the astronauts were spinning around the world at 27,300 kilometres per hour. The speed was most apparent when the sun set every 90 minutes.

But whether it was day or night didn't really matter when they were placing the parts. Powerful floodlights illuminated the great structures so that no matter what had to be done the astronauts could clearly see what they were working on. For her part, Julie successfully operated the mechanical arms with precision and confidence. She directed Canadarm2 to lift "Jeff" out of the cargo bay of the shuttle. And later she used Canadarm to take "Jelly" from the same place. She also operated the third arm, the Japanese-American one.

Julie Payette and Bob Thirsk on the International Space Station. This was the first time two Canadians had ever met in space.

But for Julie, meeting with Bob Thirsk was particularly enjoyable. Just to be able to see and talk to another Canadian on the station was so unique; she knew she would not forget the occasion. Both astronauts are wonderful representatives for their country, and just by being together in perhaps the most unusual location imaginable made them historical figures for a space-faring nation.

Julie, whose goal is excellence in everything she does, could not have been more thrilled to do what she had done. She overcame so many obstacles before she became an ambassador in the sky. Back when she applied to become an astronaut,

FASCINATING FACT
The First Canadian in Charge of the ISS

In 2012, Chris Hadfield will become the first Canadian commander of the International Space Station. Chris will be on the station for six months, and be commander for the last three months of his mission. Like Bob Thirsk, he will travel there in a Russian Soyuz. As of this writing, his launch date is tentatively scheduled for December 2012.

even she could not have imagined how far her career would take her. For that reason, she believes in a future where other Canadians will do even greater things in space. Like her, they will be the boys and girls who dare to dream, who want to do great things for their country, and who have the courage to work hard to do so. When Julie applied to be as astronaut, even though she was young, Canada didn't even *have* astronauts. She knew, of course, that she might have a chance. On the other hand, she knew that if she didn't apply she had no chance of having her dreams come true. She sent in her application as soon as she could.

Finally, all the objectives of STS-127 were complete. The *Endeavour* crew said goodbye to the space station crew and prepared to back away. Julie Payette closed the hatch prior to departure and assisted as the pilot undocked the shuttle. There was a last fly-around as station members took photos of *Endeavour*, to check that there was no damage to the exterior of the shuttle. Had any tiles or anything else not checked out, a decision would have been made right away about to how to deal with the matter. No one on board wanted to face the heat of entering the Earth's atmosphere unless all aspects of the shuttle were problem free. Fortunately, all was well.

Endeavour's return to Earth went exactly as planned. The skies were sunny in Florida when the shuttle appeared as a tiny speck in the northern sky. Shortly before 11:00 in the morning, the crowd of well-wishers who had gathered to watch the touchdown cheered as the spacecraft approached. In no time, it was sitting on the Kennedy Space Center runway and Mission Control was sending a radio message welcoming the crew back home.

Six Months on the Space Station

In 1984, Marc Garneau became the first Canadian to go into space. Much more recently, Dr. Bob Thirsk became the first Canadian to *live* in space. He was on the International Space Station for six months. Because Canada was one of the building nations of the ISS, Bob got to go there. His presence on board was an unforgettable experience for him, and a memorable achievement for this country. Canadians of all ages and stripes were proud of him and delighted that he was there. Many of us probably wished we could have been with him!

Perhaps someday we all will be able to live in space. You may wonder if you could be like Dr. Thirsk. None of us know what the future may bring, but it is sure to be exciting and surprising at times. As you may remember that when Bob Thirsk was a boy he was fascinated by astronauts, and hoped to be one when he grew up. He even dreamed he would live in space. If you have the same dream perhaps it will come true too.

Since the space stations have proven that we can spend long periods of time living and working in space, eventually we may be able to live and work elsewhere in the universe. Many astronauts are sure that humans will go back to the moon within a few years, and then on to the planet Mars. Maybe you will be one of the lucky individuals who will do such things. Reading about how Bob Thirsk spent his time on the ISS may give you some idea of how wonderful it

FASCINATING FACT
Learning Russian

Bob Thirsk is not only a husband, a father, and an astronaut; among other things he is also an engineer, a medical doctor, and a hockey player. But there is one thing he does not claim to be: he is not a master of many languages. He speaks English and French fluently, but found that learning Russian was particularly difficult for him. He eventually mastered that language, but only after much study, and hard work.

would be to travel off Earth and live somewhere far above the clouds for a long period of time. As we know, Bob Thirsk did just that.

Bob had to do many things before this flight. He trained at the Johnson Space Center, of course — but he also went to Russia to train. While he was there he also used the time to improve his Russian, study the Russian spacesuits and other equipment, the procedures used there, and particularly to become familiar with the Soyuz, the spaceship flown by the Russians. While none of these things was easy, they were all necessary. The Soyuz, for example, is quite different from the American space shuttle. And while it may be old, crude, and uncomfortable now, it is reliable, and has taken many men and women into space and brought them back. It takes off in much the same way as the shuttle does, but on return it floats to Earth under a parachute.

In Russia, astronauts are called cosmonauts. There is room for three cosmonauts in the Soyuz. The part of the spaceship used for launch and landing is bullet shaped, and is called a re-entry module. Once in space, the cosmonauts ride in an egg-shaped section of the machine known as an orbital module. That part is slightly larger, but still only about as wide as the inside of a car. Those who fly in the Soyuz sit side by side. In pictures they look as if they're really cramped together. Nevertheless, the machine performs well, and that is what matters most. It certainly mattered to Bob Thirsk as he settled into his position for launch on May 27, 2009. The fiery liftoff was at the Baikonur Spaceport in Kazakhstan, where all Russian spaceships depart.

The launch was televised, and many in Canada watched. Dr. Thirsk wore a white spacesuit with blue trim and his name on the front, just below his chin. A Canadian flag patch was on his left arm. In the pictures on television, he looked happy, perhaps a bit nervous, but relieved to be leaving. Two days later, he was at the space station. For the next six months, he was

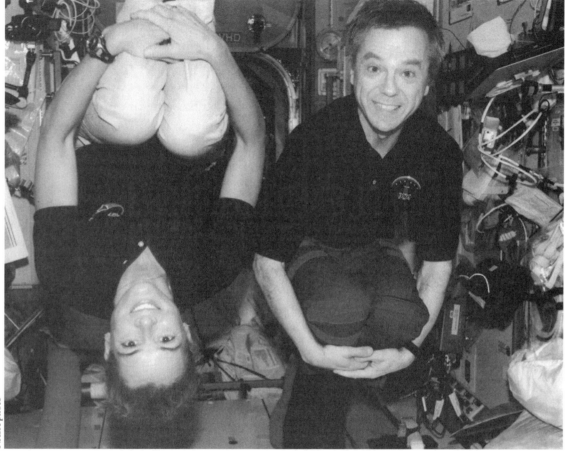

Julie Payette and Bob Thirsk pose together during their time on the International Space Station. Which way is up?

both medical officer and engineer. During his time on the station, six astronauts lived there full-time. In the past, as the place was being built, there had been room for just three.

Life on the station is a bit like life on the shuttle — except there's more room and nothing is as rushed as it is on the shuttle. Shuttle flights last only a week or two; on the station there is a lot more time. But even though there is more room, there is never complete privacy — though the extra room is very welcome for astronauts used to being in cramped space. The interior of the ISS is about the size of three Canadian houses, but with six people living there, and more visiting when shuttles arrived, some crowding occurs.

Meal preparation times have to be carefully scheduled, as does time on the two space-to-ground communication channels. Naturally, everyone wants to have their own time to link with Earth. Co-operative timelines have to be followed to make sure everyone gets time to use exercise equipment. Each astronaut on the station has to exercise for at least two hours a day. There's good reason for that.

The more time humans spend in space, the more their bodies deteriorate. Every member of what was officially called Expedition 20/21 understood this, and did their best to counteract it. The problem is with their bones in particular. Every hour of every day in orbit meant the loss of calcium from bones. Since bones are what support our weight, *any* bone loss is bothersome. A new type of exercise machine was tried on the ISS, but it is not yet known how much it helped. Bob and some of his crewmates took medication to try and prevent as much bone loss as possible, but the long-term results have yet to be determined.

This specific problem has received a great deal of attention, especially because if human beings go to other planets, they will spend much longer periods of time — even years — in space. Even now, some astronauts who have returned from the space station have been unable to walk for several hours. Fortunately, after they are back on Earth and used to gravity again, they grow stronger, and eventually return to normal. If medical problems become too serious, extended space voyages might not be possible. That's why scientists and other space experts are working hard to solve these kinds of medical problems. Bob Thirsk is one of them.

Every day during his six months on the station, Bob worked to try to understand the difficulties astronauts face. He also did what he could to study medical problems that occur on

Earth. He conducted experiments on how humans could overcome balance problems, particularly as they affect older people. Most of us know about someone who fell and injured themselves because they lost their balance. Bob knew that if he could find a way to prevent such accidents, he would be helping us all. He also tried to learn as much as he could about why human beings get dizzy and fall, or have fainting spells and fall. He also worked on experiments to improve the treatment of heart disease, and many other things.

There were also "space projects" that interested Bob.

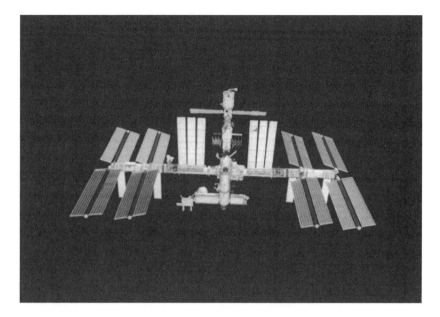

The International Space Station is huge. *It is longer than a football field and its mass would be about the same as 330 cars piled together.*

NASA photo

One involved a thing that looked a bit like a little toy truck. In fact, it was a robot that was located at the Canadian Space Agency facility, just south of Montreal. The little four-wheeled vehicle is a model for something that might be used on Mars or other new planets that humans explore. Bob used radio signals to control the device remotely, similar to the toy trucks some of us have played with here on Earth, but much more complicated. The robot is just one of many devices that are being tested for use by space travellers in the future.

Being on the station was not all work. In fact, many aspects of being there were really special. For example, Bob had looked forward to seeing Canada in a whole new way, and over a period of many months. Because the station orbit is often over Canada, Bob was able to not

FASCINATING FACT
The Canadian Space Tourist

Julie Payette visited Bob Thirsk at the International Space Station, but she was not the only Canadian to do so. The other person was a man who is neither an astronaut nor a cosmonaut. His name is Guy Laliberté, and he's the founder of Cirque de Soleil, an entertainment company based in Quebec. Mr. Laliberté paid the Russians several million dollars to take him to the space station. While he was there, he conducted a series of concerts that were broadcast live on the Internet, and were seen in countries around the world. He said he did so in order to help raise awareness of the increasing scarcity of water on Earth.

only see his homeland, but to see it change. He saw the green leaves of summer turn to red and yellow in the fall, and then disappear from the trees as winter approached. He saw open water on lakes and in what seemed like no time saw those lakes become ice. He saw farmland that was green in summer, rust and gold when wheat and other crops were ripe, and grey black when ploughed in the fall. These things were all interesting, wonderful, and truly beautiful.

But Bob Thirsk missed his home, of course, and his family. He had his 56th birthday in space, and knew it would be one that he would remember always. His crewmates wished him a happy birthday, but it was not quite the same as being able to hug his three children and share the time with his wife, Brenda. Bob was also concerned about the long-term effects being in space would have on his health. Nevertheless, whatever the future held, he knew in his heart that getting the chance to spend time on the space station was a joy and a privilege very few ever get. He worked hard while he was there, and was satisfied that he had done everything he could have done to succeed and bring credit to himself and his homeland.

When the Soyuz that was taking him home arrived, Bob had mixed feelings about his entire adventure. He looked around the station, visited all of the rooms for the last time, and said goodbye to the crew members he was leaving behind. Then, with a final glance around the marvelous home he would never live in again, he and two others moved into the Russian rocket and prepared for departure. Two days later, they touched the good Earth again.

The trip back from space was routine. On Tuesday, December 1, 2009, the spacecraft landed on an open plain in Kazakhstan. Bob and the two men with him were all glad to be back. Steve MacLean, who is now president of the Canadian Space Agency, was there to welcome the travellers, and to congratulate Bob on a fantastic voyage. A short time later the three spacemen were removed from the Soyuz and placed in all-terrain vehicles. Helicopters, which generally pick up those returning from space, were unable to fly because of freezing temperatures and low cloud that blanketed the immediate area. However, after a short trail trip, the vehicles brought the travellers to an airport where they transferred to planes and flew to reunions with loved ones. For Bob Thirsk, the only Canadian to live and work on the International Space Station, a memorable journey was over.

Epilogue:
Canada's Future in Space

On Wednesday, May 13, 2009, two new Canadian astronauts were named. One is a medical doctor; the other a fighter pilot. The doctor is David St. Jacques of Quebec City, and the pilot is Jeremy Hansen from London, Ontario.

The two men were chosen from the 5,351 people who applied — and were the first additions to the Canadian astronaut group in 17 years. After being selected they spent several weeks at the Canadian Space Agency, and then left for training at the Johnson Space Center at Houston, Texas. The two men will continue and add to the legacy left by the outstanding individuals who came before them.

References

Books and Magazines

Bondar, Barbara and Dr. Roberta Bondar. *On the Shuttle: Eight Days in Space.* Toronto: Greey de Pencier, 1993.

Bondar, Roberta. *Touching the Earth.* Toronto: Key Porter, 1994.

Dixon, Joan. *Roberta Bondar: The Exceptional Achievements of Canada's First Woman Astronaut.* Canmore, AB: Altitude Publishing Canada, Ltd., 2004.

Dotto, Lydia. *The Astronauts: Canada's Voyageurs in Space.* Toronto: Stoddart, 1993.

____. *Canada in Space.* Toronto: Irwin Publishing, 1987.

Gainor, Chris. *Canada in Space: The People and Stories Behind Canada's Role in the Exploration of Space.* Edmonton: Folklore Publishing, 2006.

Glover, Linda K. *National Geographic Encyclopedia of Space.* Washington: National Geographic, 2005.

Goodwin, Robert. *Space Shuttle Fact Archive.* Burlington, ON: Apogee Books, 2007.

Gorn, Michael and Buzz Aldrin. *NASA: The Complete Illustrated History.* New York: Merrell, 2005.

Kitmacher, Gary, ed. *Reference Guide to the International Space Station*. Burlington, ON: Apogee Books, 2006.

Melady, John. *Canadians in Space: The Forever Frontier*. Toronto: Dundurn, 2009.

Owen, David. *Final Frontier: Voyages into Outer Space*. Richmond Hill, ON: Firefly, 2003.

Ross-Nazzal, Jennifer. "The Right Place: Houston Makes History." *Houston History*, Volume 6, Number 1, Fall 2008.

Spangenburg, Ray and Kit Moser. *On Board the Space Shuttle*. New York: Franklin Watts, 2002.

Websites

Canadian Space Agency: *www.space.gc.ca*

European Space Agency: *www.esa.int*

Johnson Space Center: *www.spacecenter.org*

Kennedy Space Center: *www.kennedyspacecenter.com*

NASA Human Spaceflight: *www.spaceflight.nasa.gov*

National Aeronautics and Space Administration: *www.nasa.gov*

Russian Federal Space Agency: *www.roscosmos.ru*

Spaceflight Now: *www.spaceflightnow.com*

Acknowledgements

No book about astronauts will ever be complete. That's because the world in which they work changes constantly. There are always new missions, new discoveries, and new problems to be solved. Shuttle and Soyuz flights are never the same. Crews change, objectives change, and even the dangers change. This little book is an attempt to tell their stories.

This volume follows on my *Canadians in Space*, and many of the same individuals and organizations deserve my thanks. I am indebted in particular to the astronauts for their time and their insight. I felt privileged to be able to talk with so many of them. NASA and Canadian Space Agency representatives were all helpful, as were the personnel I was privileged to deal with in Washington, Longueuil, Houston, and Cape Canaveral. I am grateful as well to Kirk Howard, Michael Carroll, Jennifer Scott for the design of the book, Cheryl Hawley for her editing skills, and to the wonderful sales people at Dundurn. But most of all, as always, to Mary.

John Melady
Seaforth, Ontario

Index

BY THE SAME AUTHOR

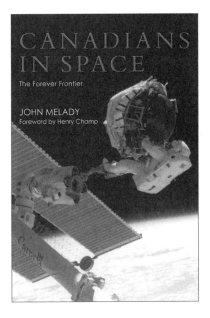

Canadians in Space
The Forever Frontier
John Melady
978-1-550029406
$27.99

On October 5, 1984, Marc Garneau became Canada's first astronaut when he rocketed into space from a launch pad at Cape Canaveral, Florida. In doing so, Garneau became a national hero. Seven of his fellow citizens followed in his footsteps, many more than once. Julie Payette, a young mother and adventurer from Montreal was the first Canadian woman to visit the International Space Station. Chris Hadfield, a former fighter pilot from Ontario, was the first Canadian to do a spacewalk, while Saskatchewan-born Doctor Dave Williams performed surgery on test animals while his shuttle sped around the globe.

This book was written as a 25th anniversary tribute to these brave men and women who defied tremendous odds, risked their lives, and soared from earth on sheets of flame. By leaving the only planet known to be habitable, they became true explorers in an ever-expanding universe we will never completely know.

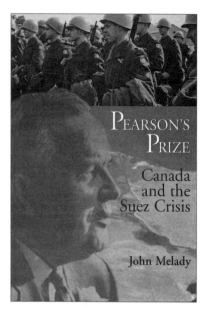

Pearson's Prize

John Melady

978-1- 550026115

$30.00

In the fall of 1956, the world was on the brink of war. Egyptian President Gamel Nasser nationalized the Suez Canal, and Britain, France, and Israel attacked him. Russia supported Nasser, and Soviet Premier Khrushchev threatened nuclear holocaust if the United States became militarily involved. Soon, the matter became a major problem for the United Nations.

Fortunately, because of the efforts of Lester Pearson, then Canada's minister of External Affairs, the crisis was defused. Pearson proposed a U.N. peacekeeping force be sent to Egypt to separate the warring factions there and keep the peace. Because his idea was adopted, Pearson helped save the world from war. For his outstanding states-manship, Pearson won the Nobel Prize for Peace, the only Canadian ever to do so. This book, written to commemorate the fiftieth anniversary of the event, is about the Suez and about Pearson's work during a tension-filled time in the twentieth century.

Available at your favourite bookseller.

 **DUNDURN PRESS**
www.dundurn.com

What did you think of this book?
Visit www.dundurn.com for reviews, videos, updates, and more!